# A MARATHI
# REFERENCE GRAMMAR

# MARATHI TEACHING MATERIALS

*An Intermediate Marathi Reader, Parts 1 and 2*
*An Advanced Marathi Reader, Parts 1 and 2*
*A Basic Marathi–English Dictionary*
*A Marathi Reference Grammar*

## Maxine Berntsen and Jai Nimbkar

# A MARATHI
# REFERENCE GRAMMAR

**MAXINE BERNTSEN**
**JAI NIMBKAR**

South Asia Regional Studies
University of Pennsylvania, Philadelphia

# A MARATHI REFERENCE GRAMMAR
1975

Printed in India by C. S. LATKAR, Kalpana Mudranalaya, 461-4 Shiv-Parvati, Tilak Road, Poona 30 and published by RICHARD D. LAMBERT, Department of South Asia Regional Studies, University of Pennsylvania, Philadelphia, Pennsylvania, 19174, U.S.A.

The research reported herein was performed pursuant to a contract with the U.S. Department of Health, Education and Welfare, Office of Education, under the authority of Title VI, Section 602, NDEA.

# Preface

Adult students learning Marathi through the medium of English have long felt the need for a manual setting forth the basic grammatical facts of the language. This book is an attempt to meet that need.

The appearance of formulas in these pages should not frighten off the prospective user of the book. The formulas are simple, and experience has shown that most students find them helpful. The reason is that a formula can show an abstract pattern in all its clarity. However, if a particular student feels intimidated by the formulas he can always ignore them and concentrate on the examples.

The grammatical outline presented here is based on the model of transformational grammar developed at the University of Pennsylvania by Zellig Harris. We feel that this particular model is expecially well-suited for giving the student a sense of the structure of the language.

This book can be used in various ways. The majority of students will use it only as a reference volume to check particular facts. However, the student who takes the trouble to read through the whole book will get more out of it.

Though the book is aimed particularly at students of Marathi, we hope it will be of interest to linguists as well. Since many examples have been given, linguists will have ample scope to do their own analyses of the materials.

We feel confident in the validity of overall structure of this book and in the accuracy of the examples given. At the same time, we are conscious of the imperfections in the treatment of some grammatical details. Whatever its imperfections, however, we hope the book will be of use.

Phaltan/District Satara
Maharashtra, India

Maxine Berntsen
Jai Nimbkar

# Acknowledgments

The writing of this book has been made possible by the cooperation of several institutions and individuals. The original manuscript was prepared as part of a contract with the American Peace Corps for the production of Marathi teaching materials. It was revised and expanded as part of a contract with the US Office of Education for production of a set of intermediate and advanced Marathi teaching materials. The contract was between the Office of Education and the University of Pennsylvania. It was administered in India by the American Institute of Indian Studies and carried out under the auspices of the Deccan College. Special thanks are due to Dr. Julia A. Petrov of the Office of Education, Dr. Richard D. Lambert of the University of Pennsylvania, and Dr. A. M. Ghatage of the Deccan College.

In planning the revision of the grammar we found a number of useful suggestions in Franklin C. Southworth's *A Student's Hindi–Urdu Reference Manual*. For some grammatical points we consulted Ashok R. Kelkar's *The Phonology and Morphology of Marathi* and Damle's *Shāstriya marāṭhī vyākaraṇ*. Naresh B. Kavadi and Franklin C. Southworth's *Spoken Marathi*, H. M. Lambert's *Marathi Language Course*, and Rev. Alfred Darby's *A Primer of the Marathi Language for the Use of Adults* were also helpful.

The task of checking and proofreading was considerably lightened by the competent work of Ku. Nandini Nimbkar. English typing was done by Shri. N. G. Phadke, Marathi typing by Ku. Nalini Gangal. Printing was done by C. S. Latkar of the Kalpana Mudranalaya.

# Contents

Tables

Figures

# SIGNS AND ABBREVIATIONS

| | | | |
|---|---|---|---|
| A | adjective | M | morphophonemic |
| adj. | adjective | n. | neuter |
| adv. | adverb | N | noun |
| Aux | auxiliary | neg. | negative |
| C | consonant | obl. | oblique |
| cf. | compare | opt. | optional |
| conj. | conjunction | p. | person |
| d | desiderative | ph | past habitual |
| E | ending | perf. | perfect |
| Eng. | English | pl. | plural |
| excl. | exclusive | post. | postposition |
| f | future | prep. | preposition |
| f. | feminine | respect. | respectful |
| f. (e) | feminine, (e) class | S | sentence |
| f. (i) | feminine, (i) class | sg. | singular |
| fam. | familiar | sing. | singular |
| hab | habitual | sp. | special |
| hon. | honorific | str. | straight |
| i. e. | that is | subjunct | subjunctive |
| imf | imperfect | V | verb |
| imp | imperative | $V_w$ | vowel |
| impers. | impersonal | v.i. | intransitive verb |
| incl. | inclusive | v.t. | transitive verb |
| K | question word | var. | variant |
| m. | masculine | → | becomes |

# Chapter one

# THE MARATHI SOUND SYSTEM

## A. General Introduction: the Production of Speech Sounds

### 1. Vocal tract

Speech is produced by a series of muscular adjustments made on a column of air expelled from the lungs during the process of breathing. The vocal tract, in which these adjustments are made, has four main areas: the larynx, the pharynx, the oral cavity, and the nasal cavity, as shown in Fig. 1.

**The larynx.** The larynx is a cartilaginous structure, the outer part of which protrudes in the throat, and is called the Adam's apple. Inside the larynx is a passage for air, with two lip–like membranes, the vocal cords, fitting across it. In normal breathing, unaccompanied by speech, the vocal cords are relaxed and slightly apart, so that air can pass through them with little or no sound. When the vocal cords are completely closed, the air–flow is cut off altogether, producing an abrupt sound like that uttered by a person with a sudden, sharp stitch of pain. When tightened without closure, the cords vibrate. This vibration, known as *voicing*, is the fundamental speech sound.

You can get an idea of what voicing is by putting your fingers on your Adam's apple. First simply breathe; you can feel no movement in the larynx. Then hum up the scale; now you should be able to feel the vibration in the larynx.

The speech sound produced on one burst of air is a *syllable*. Since voicing is necessary for speeeh sound, at least a portion of every syllable must be voiced. By variations in the timing of its tensing and relaxing in relation to the upper areas of the vocal tract, the larynx can assist in producing a variety of sounds.

**The pharynx ( throat ).** The pharynx can be left completely open so that air

1

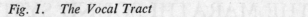

*Fig. 1.   The Vocal Tract*

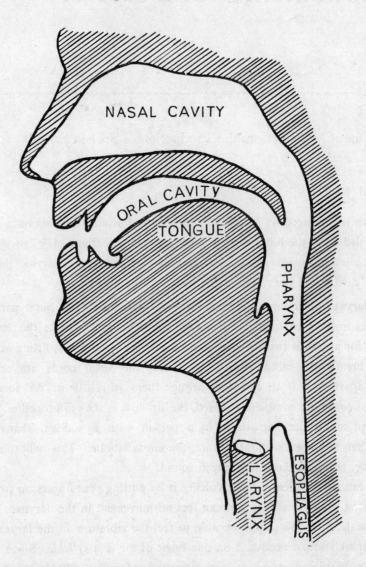

This figure is adapted from Charles F. Hockett, *A Course in Modern Linguistics* (New York: Macmillan, 1958). This entire introduction is largely based on Hockett's presentation.

may pass through it freely, or it may be partially or wholly closed by retracting the root of the tongue until it makes contact with the pharyngeal wall.

**The nasal cavity**. The fleshy piece hanging down in the back of the mouth is the *uvula*. The back part of the uvula, known as the *velic*, serves as a valve controlling the flow of air into the nasal cavity. If the velic is raised until it touches the pharyngeal wall, the nasal cavity is closed off. In this case the sound produced is completely *oral*, i. e., produced in the mouth. If the velic is open some of the air passes into the nasal cavity, and the sound is *nasal* or *nasalized*.

**The oral cavity ( mouth )**. It is in the mouth that the greatest number of articulations are possible. The musculature of the tongue, lips, and face, acting on the bony surfaces of the teeth, the alveolar ridge ( the bony ridge behind the teeth ), and the palate can modify the size and shape of the resonance chamber, and thus create a great variety of sounds. Further modifications are made possible by the horizontal or lateral action of the jaw.

The sounds produced in the mouth can be divided basically into two types: those in which the air passes through unimpeded ( vowels ) and those in which the air is wholly or partially stopped ( consonants ).

## 2. Vowels

Generally speaking, all vowels are voiced. They differ from each other primarily in the shape of the resonance chamber created in the mouth. These shape differences are primarily determined by differences in tongue height. The conventionalized diagram below shows the approximate tongue positions for the major vowels.

|  |  | High |  |  |
|---|---|---|---|---|
|  | i | ɨ | u |  |
| Front | e | ə | o | Back |
|  | ɛ |  |  |  |
|  | æ |  | ɔ |  |
|  |  | a |  |  |
|  |  | Low |  |  |

*English examples*

| | | | | | | |
|---|---|---|---|---|---|---|
| i | as in | b*eet* | ə | as in | b*u*t |
| e | as in | b*ai*t | a | as in | f*a*ther |
| ɛ | as in | b*e*t | u | as in | b*oo*t |
| æ | as in | b*a*t | o | as in | b*oa*t |
| ɨ | not in Eng. | | ɔ | as in | b*ough*t |

There are also factors other than tongue height which differentiate vowels. One factor is length—that is, the amount of time the vowel is held. Closely related to length is a second factor—the degree of muscular tension. Another factor is the constancy of the position of the tongue during the production of the vowel. This is an important difference between Marathi and English vowels. In Marathi most vowels are ' pure; ' that is, the tongue is held in the same position and the vowel consequently has the same value throughout its duration. In most English vowels the position of the tongue shifts slightly during the articulation of the vowel, producing what is called a *glide*. You will notice that if you listen closely to the vowel in English *bait* ( phonetically / bet / ) the *e* is followed by a short *y* sound. Similarly, the *o* in *boat* is actually *o*ʷ. While learning Marathi English speakers must learn to pronounce vowels without a glide.

## 3. Consonants

Consonants may vary according to articulation ( articulator, place and manner of articulation ), position of the velic, and position of the larynx.

There are three principal manners of articulation: stop, continuant and spirant ( or fricative ). In a stop, the air-flow is completely impeded, as in the final *p* of the word *stop*. In a continuant, the air-flow is not wholly impeded, so the sound can continue until all air is expelled. Vowels and nasals are all continuants; *l* also is, because while the air-flow is stopped in the center by the tip of the tongue, it can still pass freely on both sides of the tongue. In a spirant the air-flow is impeded but not stopped entirely, and the resulting friction is audible, as in the *f* of *first* or the *s* of *bus*. An *affricate* is a combination of a stop and a spirant; it begins with a stop and ends with a spirant; like the *ch* of *church* or the *ts* of *spots*.

The two principal articulators are the tongue and the lips.

**Tongue.** For purposes of articulatory description the tongue is usually divided into three parts, as seen in Fig. 2.

Fig. 2.   The Tongue

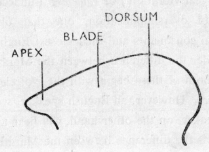

The articulations of the tongue and the lips are summarized in Table 1.1.

Table 1.1.    *Articulations of Tongue and Lips*

| Articulator | Area made contact with | Name of sound |
|---|---|---|
| **Tongue** | | |
| ( a ) tip | teeth | dental |
| tip | alveolar ridge | alveolar |
| tip | center of palate* | retroflex |
| ( b ) blade | palate | palatal |
| ( c ) back | back of palate ( velum ) | dorsal–velar |
| ( dorsum ) | | |
| **Lower lip** | | |
| | upper lip | labial |
| | teeth | labio–dental |

**Position of the velic.**   If the velic is open, the air flows into the nasal cavity, producing a nasal sound.   Most stops and spirants have a corresponding nasal; that is, the articulator and place of articulation are the same; the resonance chamber is different. ( Say, for instance, *be, me*; in both words the lips come together in the same way. ) Moreover, since the air–flow is impeded in the mouth but free to resonate in the nasal cavity until it is expended, nasal sounds are continuants.

*Normally the tip of the tongue makes contact with the teeth or the alveolar ridge. In order for it to touch the center of the palate, the lower jaw must be thrust forward. The sound is called retroflex ( 'turned back' ) because the tongue makes contact further back than normal.

**Laryngeal position**. Conventionally, consonants are described as *voiced* ( accompanied by laryngeal vibration ) or *voiceless* ( unaccompanied by laryngeal vibration ). This is an oversimplification, one that obscures the difference between certain Marathi consonants and their closest English counterparts. For instance, we may consider the difference between the Marathi syllable *pə* and the English syllable *pə*. Both of these begin with the voiceless bilabial *p* and end with the neutral vowel *ə*. However, an English speaker will hear the Marathi *pə* as *bə*. The Marathi speaker, on the other hand, will hear an English word—initial *pə* as *phə*. What, then, is the difference between the Marathi and the English *pə* ? The difference comes in the timing of the laryngeal hum. In the Marathi syllable, the larynx is tense, and voicing begins almost immediately. In the English syllable, the larynx is more relaxed, and an audible puff of air called *aspiration*, is allowed to escape before voicing begins. If the larynx is very tense, and voicing begins simultaneously with the closure of the lips, the sound is clearly voiced, as in the Marathi *bə*. In an English *bə* the onset of the voicing is slightly delayed, so that it sounds very much like a Marathi *pə*.

To sum up, then, we may visualize the Marathi and English bilabial sounds on a continuum.* At the left end the larynx is initially relaxed. As we move to the right the onset of laryngeal tension starts earlier.

— — — — — — — — — — — — — —→

Mar. *phə* Eng. *pə* ( *initial* ) Mar. *pə* Eng. *bə* Mar. *bə*

If the larynx is initially tense, and the air pressure is increased so that audible friction is produced as air passes through the larynx, the sound is a *voiced aspirate*.

Since voicing implies laryngeal tension and aspiration generally implies relaxation, a voiced aspirate sounds like a contradiction in terms. Apparently, however, the great increase in air pressure makes possible the passage of air through the partially—closed larynx. Voiced aspirates are not found in English, but in the Marathi sound system there is a full series of them: *gh, jh, ḍh, dh* and *bh*.

## 4. How do the sound systems of languages vary ?

All normal people have the same physiological equipment for sound production.

*The discussion of voicing presented here is a somewhat simplified version of the views of Lisker and Abramson in L. Lisker and and A. Abramson, " A Cross—Language Study of Voicing in Initial Stops: Acoustical Measurement. *Word* 20,384–422.

How, then, do the sound systems of languages vary? The differences lie in four areas:

( a ) Selection of articulations. No language uses all possible articulations. Certain articulations, such as bilabial stops, are almost universal; others, like pharyngeal stops, are fairly rare.

( b ) Phonetic detail of 'same' articulation. We have already seen an example of this in the discussion of Marathi and English *p* and *b*.

( c ) Fitting of articulations into a system. In every language many articulations are used, and their interrelations are very complex. However, language is an economical and efficient signalling system because only a small number of features are selected as significant. The listener attends to only the significant features: is it voiced? is it dental? The set of significant features differs from one language to another. In English there are aspirated stops, but the feature of aspiration is not significant. In Marathi, however, there are pairs of words in which the only difference is that one is aspirated and one is not. Thus aspiration is significant in Marathi.

( d ) Permitted sound sequences. Each language has its own rules governing the permitted sound sequences. A perfectly familiar sound may be hard to pronounce if it occurs in a position different from what a person is used to.

## B.  The Marathi Sound System

### 1. Vowels

Marathi has the following vowels and diphthongs ( combinations of two vowels ).

$$ə \quad \bar{ə} \quad a \quad \breve{\imath} \quad \bar{\imath} \quad \breve{u} \quad \bar{u} \quad ɨ \quad e \quad əi \quad o \quad əu$$

A contrast between short and long *i* and between short and long *u* occurs only in a few words borrowed from Sanskrit. Otherwise both vowels are long except when followed by two consonants.[*]

---

[*] The matter is actually a great deal more complicated than this, but a student can perhaps best master subtle variations in vowel length by imitation of a native speaker. For a detailed discussion of the factors affecting vowel length, see Ashok R. Kelkar, *The Phonology and Morphology of Marathi* ( Ithaca: Cornell University Dissertation: 1958 ), p. 21.

| | |
|---|---|
| pĭ- | drink |
| pĭp | water cask |
| pĭmpəḷ | kind of tree |
| būt | shoe |
| bŭṭka | short |

Since the difference between short and long *i* and *u* is automatically determined, this text will not indicate length for them.

There is a contrast between short and long *ə* only at the end of a word. The short *ə* is actually the automatic result of certain consonant combinations; the long *ə* is the normal vowel *ə*. In this text long *ə* in word-final position will be written *ə*: .

bəndə

bhaṇḍə:

With the exceptions just mentioned, Marathi vowels are always pronounced long.

## 2. Consonants

The Marathi consonants are listed in Table 1.2. Note that for each of the five main articulatory positions — back, palatal, retroflex, dental, and labial — there are five sounds: voiceless unaspirate, voiceless aspirate, voiced unaspirate, voiced aspirate, and nasal. The last line of the table contains semivowels and other miscellaneous sounds which do not fit in the above pattern.

Table 1.2.    *Marathi Consonants*

| | Voiceless | | Voiced | | Nasal |
|---|---|---|---|---|---|
| | Unaspirated | Aspirated | Unaspirated | Aspirated | |
| Back | k | kh | g | gh | ŋ |
| Palatal | c ( ts ) | čh | j ( dz ) | jh | ñ |
| | č | | ǰ | ǰh | |
| Retroflex | ṭ | ṭh | ḍ | ḍh | ṇ |
| Dental | t | th | d | dh | n |
| Labial | p | ph | b | bh | m |
| | y r l v š s h ḷ | | | | |

According to the convention for transcribing Marathi, *ts* will be transcribed as *c*, and *dz* as *j*. There is no contrast between *c* and *č*, or between *j* and *ǰ*, before *i*. In this position *c* → *č* and *j* → *ǰ*. The same shift is optional before *e*. Among non—standard speakers the rule is extended to *s* also: *s* → *š* before *i, e*.

## 3. Difficulties for English speakers

Six kinds of Marathi consonants present special difficulties for English speakers:

( a ) voiceless unaspirate
( b ) voiced aspirate
( c ) contrast between dental and retroflex
( d ) *r*
( e ) *v*
( f ) *ts* and *dz*

**Voiceless unaspirates.** As we have seen earlier, English initial *p, t, k* are aspirated. You can get a vivid demonstration of that by putting a lighted match in front of your mouth and saying *Pete*. If you have lined the match up right it goes out. You can consider the *p* of *Pete* as equivalent to the Marathi aspirate *ph*. Similarly, an initial English *k* as in *kick* is equivalent to Marathi *kh*. What you have to work on are the unaspirated sounds. These require tension in the larynx, and for the *p*, in the lips. For the *k* the tension is in the larynx and at the back of the tongue. Try to say *p, k* with a lighted match in front of your mouth. If it goes out from your puff of air, you have failed to cut out the aspiration.

**Voiced aspirates.** Voiced aspirates, as we have seen, are not found in English and the English speaker will find them difficult. To produce a *bhə*, first say *bəhə*, then take out the first *ə*. This requires an extra amount of air pressure from the chest. Try the same procedure for *gh*.

**Contrast between dental and retroflex.** English *t* and *d* are alveolar, that is, about halfway between the position for the Marathi dental *t* and the retroflex *ṭ*. Neither the dental nor the retroflex sounds pose any real articulatory difficulties; it is just that English speakers are not used to making or hearing the dental / retroflex contrast. To make a dental *t* or *d*, press your tongue firmly against your teeth. To make a retroflex *ṭ*, thrust your lower jaw forward and put the tip of your tongue firmly against the roof of your mouth. The sound may sound to you like *rt*, since the English *r* is a retroflex sound. When you can produce the stops, practice alternating between stop and nasal. First say a dental *t*, then *d*, then *n*, Try the same with the retroflex. Remember that the tongue position for all three sounds in each series is the same.

**Retroflex l.** The retroflex *l* ( *ḷ* ) is probably the most difficult Marathi sound for English speakers. To say *ḷ*, the speaker thrusts his lower jaw slightly forward, and flips his tongue up toward the roof of his mouth, without actually making contact with it. Try this. You may find it helpful to first practice saying *əḷə*, then shortening it to *ḷə*.

**r.** It is unfortunate that English *r* and Marathi *r* are generally represented by the same letter, because they have little similarity. The Marathi *r* is a trill; that is, the tongue is vibrated very fast against the alveolar ridge. This vibration is caused by a current of air forced under the tongue. In practicing *r* first try to imitate the sound of a motor: r r r r r r r .

**v.** English *v* is a labial dental sound. The lower lip comes in contact with the teeth. Marathi *v* is bilabial like English *w*, but the Marathi sound is a fricative. It is produced with less lip–rounding, more lip tension, and a slight amount of friction.

**c ( ts ) and j ( dz ).** These affricate sounds are a bit difficult only because they do not occur in English as unitary sounds. However, the combination *ts* occurs in such words as *bets* ( /bɛts/ ), and the combination *dz* in such words as *beds* ( /bɛdz/ ). To produce *c*, first put your tongue in the position for *t*; then without releasing it, say *sə*. Similarly, to produce *i*, first put your tongue in the position for *d*; then without releasing it, say *zə*.

**Sound sequences.** In addition to the difficulties presented by sounds not found in English, there are some difficulties caused by unfamiliar sound sequences. First of all, English speakers find it difficult to give full value to every syllable. Almost invariably they reduce vowels to *ə* when they occur in unstressed syllables. They do this because in English, vowels in unstressed syllables are usually reduced.

It is perhaps fair to say that the tendency to reduce vowels is the major fault of most English speakers of Marathi. Learning to avoid this reduction will require diligent practice.

Another aspect of Marathi sound sequencing that presents difficulties for the English speaker is the doubling of consonants. Producing a double consonant presents no articulatory difficulty; it simply means holding the tongue in contact for a moment before releasing it. To do this one must give extra stress to the syllable in which the first half of the double consonant appears. Before practicing this, one should listen to a native speaker pronouncing double consonants until one has a sense of the rhythm: STRESS, unstress. Once one has sensed the rhythm, producing the double consonant should not be difficult.

# Chapter two

# THE DEVANAGARI SCRIPT

The script in which Marathi, Hindi, and Sanskrit are written is called the Devanagari script. There are slight differences in the script depending on which language it is used for. Here, of course, we will be concerned only with the Marathi version.

The Devanagari script is syllabic; that is, each character represents a syllable. We have already seen that no syllable can be pronounced without a vowel. The consonant signs as they stand represent the consonant sound plus the vowel ə. If the consonant is followed by a vowel other than ə, the sign of that vowel must be given. A consonant at the end of a syllable ( that is, following a vowel or another consonant ) has no inherent ə.

## 1. Vowels

In the traditional order of the Devanagari script, the vowels are given first. Vowel characters have two forms: a short form used when the vowel follows a consonant, and a full form when it begins a syllable or is a complete syllable by itself. The full forms of the vowel characters are listed in Table 2.1. The last two characters in the table, the *anusvar* and the *visərgə*, are not actually vowels but are traditionally listed with the vowels. They are discussed later in this chapter.

Table 2.1.   *Vowel Characters*

अ आ इ ई उ ऊ ए ऐ
ə   a   ĭ   ī   ŭ   ū   e   əi

ओ औ अं अः
o   əu   əm   əhə

In addition to these characters there are four others which are used only rarely.

ऋ ॠ ऌ ॡ
rĭ   rī   lĭ   lī

The first two are the short and long forms of syllabic *r*. The full form of short *rĭ* is used in only two or three words, but the abbreviated form is used somewhat more frequently. The long form is used only in Sanskrit. The last two characters are the long and short forms of syllabic *l*. The short form is used in only one word: क्लृप्ती *klĭpti* 'device, contrivance.' The long form is used only in Sanskrit.

There are two styles for the full forms of ĭ, ī, ŭ, ū, e and əi. The table above presents the style in which each pair has a different basic sign: इ, उ and ए. In the other style, अ is used as the basic form for each vowel sign. This style is called the Savarkar script, after its inventor, Vinayak Savarkar. It is increasingly used in magazines and in text books, but the majority of books continue to use the older script. The Savarkar script vowel signs are presented in Table 2 2.

Table 2.2.   *Vowel Characters ( Savarkar Script )*

अ आ अि अी अु अू अे
ə   a   ĭ   ī   ŭ   ū   e

अै ओ औ अं अः
əi   o   əu   əm   əhə

## 2. Consonants

The consonants are arranged according to the system already discussed in B. 2. The consonant characters are presented in Table 2.3.

We can see from this table that each letter has only one sound, and with the exception of *sə* each sound has only one character. This fact immensely simplifies the problem of learning to read and write Marathi. The two *sə*'s are distinguished by calling ष *poṭphoḍya sə* ( with the belly split ) and श *seṇḍiphoḍya sə* ( with the tuft split ).

Table 2.3.    *Consonant Characters*

| क | ख | ग | घ | ङ |
|---|---|---|---|---|
| kə | khə | gə | ghə | ŋə |
| च | छ | ज | झ | ञ |
| cə(tsə) | chə | jə(zə) | jhə | ñə |
| čə |  | ǰə | j̆hə |  |
| ट | ठ | ड | ढ | ण |
| ṭə | ṭhə | ḍə | ḍhə | ṇə |
| त | थ | द | ध | न |
| tə | thə | də | dhə | nə |
| प | फ | ब | भ | म |
| p | phə, fə | bə | bhə | mə |
| य | र | ल | व | श |
| yə | rə | lə | və | šə |
| ष | स | ह | ळ | क्ष | ज्ञ |
| šə | sə | hə | ḷə | kšə | dñe |

## 3. Abbreviated vowel signs

The full vowel characters are used only when the vowel is used without a preceding consonant, as in the following examples.

| | |
|---|---|
| आत | at |
| ऊब | ub |
| ओठ | oṭh |

When a vowel is preceded by a consonant, an abbreviated form of the vowel sign is used. The abbreviated vowel signs are presented in Table 2.4.

Table 2.4.     *Abbreviated Vowel Signs*

| अ | आ | इ | ई | उ | ऊ | ऋ |
|---|---|---|---|---|---|---|
| | ा | ि | ी | ु | ू | ृ |
| ए | ऐ | ओ | औ | अं | अः | |
| े | ै | ो | ौ | ं | ः | |

Note that there is no sign for अ, as ə is the inherent vowel in the consonant sign. The sign ा is called a *kana*, the loop on the short and long *i* is called a *velanṭi*, the loop indicating short and long *u* is called an *ukar* and the oblique line is called a *matra*. The dot is called an *anusvar* and the two dots a *visərgə*.

The examples below illustrate how the vowel signs are combined with the consonant sign क to produce syllables.

| क | का | कि | की | कु | कू | कृ |
|---|---|---|---|---|---|---|
| kə | ka | kĭ | kī | kū | kū | krĭ |

| के | कै | को | कौ | कं | कः |
|---|---|---|---|---|---|
| ke | kəi | ko | kəu | kəm | kəhə |

**Other vowels.** The long vowel ə: which occurs only at the end of a word is indicated by an *anusvar* over the preceding consonant.

*Example*

| | |
|---|---|
| भांड | bhaṇḍə: |
| केळ | keḷə: |

For loan words two additional vowel signs are used:

| | |
|---|---|
| अॅ | as in *bat* ( / bæṭ / ) |
| ऑ | as in *office* ( / ɔfis / ) |

Their abbreviated signs are : $\breve{}$ and $\breve{\imath}$ . The words above are written:

बॅट                                                    bæṭ

ऑफिस                                                  ɔfis

**Irregularities.**   र and ह have slight irregularities.   The vowel signs for short
and long *u* are attached to the middle of र.

रु                                                    r͝u

रू                                                    r‾u

Occasionally the signs are written below: रु, रू. Note that the short *u* sign has
no hook and that it curves back to the left.

The sign for *ri* is similarly put in the middle of ह.

हृ                                                    hrɪ

## 4.  Barakhədi

The table of the consonant characters with their accompanying vowel signs  is
called the *barakhədi*. The *barakhədi* is presented in Table 2.5.   Going through it
is an excellent way of learning the script and pronunciation.

**Table 2.5.** *Barakhəḍi—Consonant and Vowel Combinations*

| | | | | | | | | | | | |
|---|---|---|---|---|---|---|---|---|---|---|---|
| क | का | कि | की | कु | कू | के | कै | को | कौ | कं | कः |
| ख | खा | खि | खी | खु | खू | खे | खै | खो | खौ | खं | खः |
| ग | गा | गि | गी | गु | गू | गे | गै | गो | गौ | गं | गः |
| घ | घा | घि | घी | घु | घू | घे | घै | घो | घौ | घं | घः |
| च | चा | चि | ची | चु | चू | चे | चै | चो | चौ | चं | चः |
| छ | छा | छि | छी | छु | छू | छे | छै | छो | छौ | छं | छः |
| ज | जा | जि | जी | जु | जू | जे | जै | जो | जौ | जं | जः |
| झ | झा | झि | झी | झु | झू | झे | झै | झो | झौ | झं | झः |
| ट | टा | टि | टी | टु | टू | टे | टै | टो | टौ | टं | टः |
| ठ | ठा | ठि | ठी | ठु | ठू | ठे | ठै | ठो | ठौ | ठं | ठः |
| ड | डा | डि | डी | डु | डू | डे | डै | डो | डौ | डं | डः |
| ढ | ढा | ढि | ढी | ढु | ढू | ढे | ढै | ढो | ढौ | ढं | ढः |
| ण | णा | णि | णी | णु | णू | णे | णै | णो | णौ | णं | णः |
| त | ता | ति | ती | तु | तू | ते | तै | तो | तौ | तं | तः |
| थ | था | थि | थी | थु | थू | थे | थै | थो | थौ | थं | थः |
| द | दा | दि | दी | दु | दू | दे | दै | दो | दौ | दं | दः |
| ध | धा | धि | धी | धु | धू | धे | धै | धो | धौ | धं | धः |
| न | ना | नि | नी | नु | नू | ने | नै | नो | नौ | नं | नः |
| प | पा | पि | पी | पु | पू | पे | पै | पो | पौ | पं | पः |
| फ | फा | फि | फी | फु | फू | फे | फै | फो | फौ | फं | फः |
| ब | बा | बि | बी | बु | बू | बे | बै | बो | बौ | बं | बः |
| भ | भा | भि | भी | भु | भू | मे | मै | भो | भौ | भं | भः |
| म | मा | मि | मी | मु | मू | मे | मै | मो | मौ | मं | मः |
| य | या | यि | यी | यु | यू | ये | यै | यो | यौ | यं | यः |
| र | रा | रि | री | रु | रू | रे | रै | रो | रौ | रं | रः |
| ल | ला | लि | ली | लु | लू | ले | लै | लो | लौ | लं | लः |
| व | वा | वि | वी | वु | बू | वे | वै | वो | वौ | वं | वः |
| श | शा | शि | शी | शु | शू | शे | शै | शो | शौ | शं | शः |
| ष | षा | षि | षी | षु | षू | षे | षै | षो | षौ | षं | षः |
| स | सा | सि | सी | सु | सू | से | सै | सो | सौ | सं | सः |
| ह | हा | हि | ही | हु | हू | हे | है | हो | हौ | हं | हः |
| ळ | ळा | ळि | ळी | ळु | ळू | ळे | ळै | ळो | ळौ | ळं | ळः |
| क्ष | क्षा | क्षि | क्षी | क्षु | क्षू | क्षे | क्षै | क्षो | क्षौ | क्षं | क्षः |
| ज्ञ | ज्ञा | ज्ञि | ज्ञी | ज्ञु | ज्ञू | ज्ञे | ज्ञै | ज्ञो | ज्ञौ | ज्ञं | ज्ञः |

# TABLE 2·6

## Basic forms of Devanagari characters

---

( 1 )  उ  उ  ऊ  अ  आ  ओ  अं  अः

( 2 )  ा  अ  आ  ओ  औ

( 3 )  ᶾ  ऐ  ओ  औ

( 4 )  ड  ड  ड़  इ  ई  झ  ह

( 5 )  र  र  स

( 6 )  व  व  ब  ख  क

( 7 )  प  प  फ  ष

( 8 )　७　घ　ध　छ

( 9 )　८　ट　ठ　ढ　द

( 10 )　म　म　भ

( 11 )　य　य　थ

( 12 )　ए　ए　ऐ

## Other characters

ग　ज　ण　न　त　ळ　श　ळ　क्ष　ऋ

त्र　च　ज्ञ

## 5. Graphic analysis of Devanagari script

Learning the Devanagari script can be made easier if one first learns the basic shapes of which the characters are composed. Not every character lends itself to this analysis, but most do. The basic forms are presented in Table 2.6.

## 6. Conjunct consonants

Conjunct consonants are those that occur in a sequence without an intervening vowel. English examples are the initial sequences of *stop, trip, clip,* and the final sequences of *bunk, stump, stocked* ( phonetically *stakt* ). Since Marathi characters as they stand have an inherent *ǝ*, they must be modified in sequences where the *ǝ* is to be deleted. According to the new rules of spelling in Marathi, conjunct consonants occurring in the middle or at the end of a word are handled simply by writing the two consonants one after the other, then putting an oblique line below the first to indicate that its *ǝ* is not to be pronounced; for example: चिठ्ठी *čiṭṭhi.* This convention has still not been generally adopted, however, and traditional shapes of the conjunct consonants must be learned.

The rules for making conjunct consonants depend mostly on whether the first consonant has a vertical line from top to bottom or a short central stem from which the character is suspended.

( 1 ) Those letters which have a vertical line from top to bottom usually combine simply by omitting the line.

| | | | | | |
|---|---|---|---|---|---|
| झ | + | य | = | झ्य | jhyǝ |
| व | + | य | = | व्य | vyǝ |
| व | + | व | = | व्व | vvǝ |
| प | + | य | = | प्य | pyǝ |
| प | + | प | = | प्प | ppǝ |
| म | + | ह | = | म्ह | mhǝ |
| न | + | ह | = | न्ह | nhǝ |
| न | + | न | = | न्न | nnǝ |
| य | + | य | = | य्य | yyǝ |
| च | + | छ | = | च्छ | ččhǝ |
| घ | + | य | = | घ्य | ghyǝ |
| ध | + | य | = | ध्य | dhyǝ |
| द | + | ध | = | द्ध | ddhǝ |
| त | + | य | = | त्य | tyǝ |

| | | | | | |
|---|---|---|---|---|---|
| स | + | त | = | स्त | stə |
| स | + | स | = | स्स | ssə |
| स | + | ट | = | स्ट | stə |
| ष | + | ट | = | ष्ट | štə |
| ग | + | न | = | ग्न | gnə |

( b ) Characters suspended from a central stem have several forms. Doubling such a character is usually done by putting a truncated version of the sign beneath the full one, as in the examples below.

| | | | | | |
|---|---|---|---|---|---|
| ट | + | ट | = | ट्ट | ṭṭə |
| द | + | द | = | द्द | ddə |
| ठ | + | ठ | = | ठ्ठ | ṭṭhə |
| ड | + | ड | = | ड्ड | ḍḍə |
| ल | + | ल | = | ल्ल | llə |
| क | + | क | = | क्क | kkə |

Other combinations are handled in various ways.

| | | | | | |
|---|---|---|---|---|---|
| ट | + | य | = | ट्य | ṭyə |
| ठ | + | य | = | ठ्य | ṭhye |
| द | + | य | = | द्य | dyə |
| क | + | य | = | क्य | kyə |
| क | + | त | = | क्त | ktə |

## 7.  Special detail

( 1 ) When ल is the second character in a sequence of joint consonants, it may be written either below or after the first consonant.

| | | | | | | | |
|---|---|---|---|---|---|---|---|
| क | + | ल | = | क्ल | or | क्ल | klə |
| ब | + | ल | = | ब्ल | or | ब्ल | blə |

( 2 ) For श a special combining form श्‍ is generally used. Alternatively इ may be used.

| | | | | | | | |
|---|---|---|---|---|---|---|---|
| श | + | च | = | श्च | or | इच | ščə |
| श | + | व | = | श्व | or | इव | švə |
| श | + | ल | = | श्ल | or | इल | šlə |

( 3 ) र has several combining forms, depending on its position in the syllable and on the character it combines with.

( a ) Following another consonant

    ( i ) Consonants with right hand stem.   The र is represented by an oblique line as in the following examples.

| | | | | | |
|---|---|---|---|---|---|
| प | + | र | = | प्र | prə |
| क | + | र | = | क्र | krə |
| ब | + | र | = | ब्र | brə |
| व | + | र | = | व्र | vrə |
| श | + | र | = | श्र | šrə |

Note these special forms:

| | | | | | |
|---|---|---|---|---|---|
| त् | + | र | = | त्र | trə |
| क | + | र | = | क्र | krə |

    ( ii ) Consonants with central stem. The र is represented by the sign ∧ put below the line.

| | | | | | |
|---|---|---|---|---|---|
| ट | + | र | = | ट्र | ṭrə |
| ड | + | र | = | ड्र | ḍrə |

*Exception*

| | | | | | |
|---|---|---|---|---|---|
| द् | + | र | = | द्र | drə |

( b ) Preceding syllable–final consonant.  The र is represented by a curve called a *rəphar* put over the following consonant and its vowel sign. If the vowel sign has a *matra* or *velanṭi*, the *rəphar* goes to its right.

| | | | | | |
|---|---|---|---|---|---|
| र | + | म | = | र्म | rmə |
| र | + | व | = | र्व | rvə |
| र | + | वे | = | र्वे | rve |

Note: Actually there is no pronunciation difference between a *rəphar* and a full *r* preceding a consonant in the middle of a word. It is impossible to judge from the pronunciation which sign should be used. For such words the correct spelling must be memorized.

|  |  |
|---|---|
| पर्वत | pərvət |
| परवा | pərva |

( c ) At the beginning of syllable,  the र is represented by a curve : ˸.

| | | | | | | |
|---|---|---|---|---|---|---|
| र | + | ह | = | ᷉ह | ᷉ह्स्व | rhəsvə |
| र | + | य | = | ᷉य | दो᷉या | dorya |

## 8. Anusvar

When a nasal precedes a consonant of the same articulatory series, the nasal is represented by an *anusvar*, a dot on the character preceding the nasal. According to the new rules of writing, the nasal consonant sign is used instead of the *anusvar* in many cases. In the examples below the conventional style is shown in the first column, the new style in the second.

| | | |
|---|---|---|
| अंक | अङ्क | aηkə |
| पंखा | पङ्खा | pəηkha |
| रांग | राङ्ग | raηgə |
| चिंच | चिञ्च | čincə |
| पिंज | पिञ्ज | pinjə |
| सुंठ | सुण्ठ | suṇṭhə |
| बंड | बण्ड | bəṇḍə |
| षंढ | षण्ढ | šəṇḍhə |
| संत | सन्त | səntə |
| बंद | बन्द | bəndə |
| संप | सम्प | səmpə |
| लांब | लाम्ब | lambə |

The last seven characters of the script do not have a corresponding nasal. Note the pronunciation of the *anusvar* in each case.

| | |
|---|---|
| संयम | sə̃yyəm |
| संरक्षण | sə̃vrəksəṇ |
| संलग्न | sə̃lləgnə |
| संवाद | sə̃vsəy |
| संसार | sə̃vser |
| सिंह | sivhə |

Before य the *anusvar* is pronounced ỹ. Before ल it is pronounced l̃. Before the remaining characters — that is, र, व, श, स and ह — it is pronounced ṽ. (The sign ~ indicates slight nasalization.)

# Chapter three

# NOUNS, PRONOUNS AND ADJECTIVES

## A. Nouns

### 1. Gender

Marathi nouns are divided into three genders: masculine, feminine, and neuter. For the most part, grammatical gender has nothing to do with natural gender, and must be learned for each word.* In each gender, however, there are some nouns that have the characteristic ending of that gender. These are called *marked nouns*; all others are *unmarked*. Marked masculine nouns are those ending in *a*, marked feminine nouns those ending in *i*, and marked neuter nouns those ending in *e*. In speech the neuter *e* is regularly replaced by *ə:*. This text will treat *ə:* as the neuter ending.

Below is a summary of the possible endings of nouns in each gender class.

### Masculine

( a ) a

( b ) i ( Many of these refer to occupation, e.g.,

*maḷi* ' gardener, ' *s̆etkəri* ' farmer ' )

( c ) u

( d ) consonant

( e ) o

* Most nouns specifically referring to a male person or creature are masculine, and those specifically referring to a female creature are generally feminine. Some words referring to a person or creature without specification of sex are neuter. ( Note continued on following page. )

24

**Neuter**

( a ) ə:

( b ) i

( c ) u

( d ) consonant

**Feminine**

( a ) i

( b ) a ( Abstract nouns ending in *ta* ( ' –ness, ' ' ity ' )

are usually feminine, e.g., səkyəta ' possibility. ' )

( c ) u

( d ) consonant

( e ) o

## 2. Number, straight and oblique forms

Nouns may be either singular or plural in number. For each number there are two forms: the straight ( normal ) form, and the oblique form. The oblique form is that used before postpositions, the relational words which are like English prepositions but in Marathi follow the noun rather than precede it.

The rules for formation of plural and oblique forms in Marathi are not difficult, but they are numerous, as they vary not only for each gender but for each ending within the gender. Moreover, even words of the same gender having the same ending may fall into two or more subclasses following different rules for plural and oblique formation. And, finally, no matter how the rules are stated, there remain exceptions.

Actually, however, the situation is not as chaotic as it may seem. The majority of words do follow rules predictable from their gender and ending class. The remaining subclasses are very small, and usually consist of borrowings, especially from Sanskrit. In the following presentation we have tried to give

---

A few nouns, especially those referring to a profession or status, can be masculine or feminine ( and occasionally neuter ), depending on the person to whom they refer.

| | | |
|---|---|---|
| वकील | vəkil | lawyer |
| डॉक्टर | dɔktər | doctor |
| भाडेकरू | bhaḍekəru | renter |
| ब्राह्मण | brahməṇ | Brahman |

some indication as to which rules cover large classes and which cover small ones.

In applying the rules for formation of plural and oblique it is also necessary to apply certain general phonological rules governing word building. These are called *morphophonemic rules*. The rules are introduced at relevant places in the text, and are designated $M_1$, $M_2$, etc. They are summarized in Appendix A.

The rules for plural and oblique formation are given below.

## ( 1 ) Masculine

### (a) Marked

#### Class 1

( i ) The straight plural is formed according to the rule: *a → e.*

| | | | |
|---|---|---|---|
| रस्ता | रस्ते | rəsta | road |
| | | rəste | roads |
| हातोडा | हातोडे | hatoḍa | hammer |
| | | hatoḍe | hammers |
| हप्ता | हप्ते | həpta | installment |
| | | həpte | installments |

(ii) The oblique singular and plural is formed according to the rule: *a → ya.*

| | | |
|---|---|---|
| रस्त्यावर | rəstyavər | on the road |
| रस्त्यांवर | rəstyāvver | on the roads |
| हातोड्यानी | hatoḍyani* | with the hammer |
| हातोड्यांनी | hatoḍyanni | with the hammers |

Note that in the plural the Devanagari script has an *anusvar* ( a dot representing a nasalized sound ) over the *a* preceding the postposition. With postpositions beginning in a consonant, such as *cə:* ( possessive ), *kəḍe* ' place, ' *vər* ' on ', *na* ' to ' and *ni* ' by ' this nasal is pronounced. With other postpositions it is not pronounced, but it has been retained in writing as a convenient indication that the noun is plural.

*This can also be *hatoḍyane* or *hatoḍyanə:*. For the alternative forms of this postposition, see 6. B.

Class 2

(iii) There is a small set of masculine nouns ending in *ya.* The oblique
form of these does not change.

| वाटाड्या | vaṭaḍya | guide |
| वाटाड्याला | vaṭaḍyala | to the guide |
| वाटाड्यांना | vaṭaḍyanna | to the guides |
| पुतण्या | putəṇya | nephew |
| पुतण्याला | putəṇyala | to the nephew |
| पुतण्यांना | putəṇyanna | to the nephews |

Other words in this set include the following.

| पाणबुड्या | paṇbuḍya | diver |
| मेंढक्या | meṇḍhkya | shepherd |
| दुभाष्या | dubhaśya | interpreter |
| खवैया | khəvəiya | gourmet |

(iv) With the exception of *dubhaśya,* those words ending in *Cya** form
their plural according to the rule: *ya → e.*

| पुतण्या | putəṇya |
| पुतणे | putəṇe |
| वाटाड्या | vaṭaḍya |
| वाटाडे | vaṭaḍe |

In the case of *dubhaśya* the plural is formed regularly.

| दुभाष्या | dubhaśya |
| दुभाष्ये | dubhaśye |

( v ) Abstract nouns ending in *pəṇa* do not change in the oblique.

| मोठेपणासाठी | moṭhepəṇasaṭhi | for greatness |
| आंबटपणासाठी | ambəṭpəṇasaṭhi | for sourness |

(vi) The word *ajoba* does not change either in the plural or the
oblique.

(vii) The word *mulga* 'boy' has regular plural and oblique forms,
i. e., *mulge* and *mulgya–.* However, instead of these, the neuter
forms *mulə:* and *mula–* are generally used.

---

\* C = Consonant.

( b ) Ending in *i*

Class 1

( i ) There is no difference between the straight singular and the straight plural.

| | | |
|---|---|---|
| एक माळी | ek maḷi | one gardener |
| दोन माळी | don maḷi | two gardeners |
| एक शिंपी | ek šimpi | one tailor |
| दोन शिंपी | don šimpi | two tailors |

(ii) The oblique singular and plural for masculine nouns ending in *i* are formed according to the rule: +*a*. Rule M₁ applies: *i* and *e* become *y* before the addition of *a*.

| | | |
|---|---|---|
| माळी | maḷi | gardener |
| माळ्याला | maḷyala | to the gardener |
| माळ्यांना | maḷyanna | to the gardeners |

Class 2

(iii) There are a number of masculine nouns ending in *i* which remain unchanged in the oblique. These include the following.

| | | |
|---|---|---|
| अग्नी | əgni | fire |
| असामी | əsami | person |
| आरोपी | aropi | accused |
| कवी | kəvi | poet |
| काजी | kaji | Muslim judge |
| निधी | nidhi | fund |
| न्यायमूर्ती | nyayəmurti | judge |
| पती | pəti | husband |
| प्रतिनिधी | prətinidhi | representative |
| वादी | vadi | plaintiff |
| संधी | səndhi | sandhi |
| हत्ती | hətti | elephant |

In addition, nouns ending in the honorific *ji* do not change.

| | | |
|---|---|---|
| भाऊजी | bhauji | brother–in–law |
| गुरुजी | guruji | teacher |

( c ) Ending in *u*

( i ) There is no difference between the straight singular and the straight plural.

| एक भाऊ | ek bhau | one brother |
| दोन भाऊ | don bhau | two brothers |
| एक साधू | ek sadhu | one sadhu |
| दोन साधू | don sadhu | two sadhus |

Class 1

( ii ) Most masculine nouns ending in *u* do not change in the oblique.

| साधूला | sadhula | to the sadhu |
| साधूंना | sadhunna | to the sadhus |

Class 2

(iii) A few masculine nouns ending in *u* form the oblique singular according to the rule: + *a*, with application of Rule M$_2$: *u* and *o* become *v* before the addition of *ə*, *a*, or *e*.

| भाऊ | bhau | brother |
| भावाला | bhavala | to the brother |
| भावांना | bhavanna | to the brothers |
| गहू | gəhu | wheat |
| गव्हाला* | gəvhala | for the wheat |

Some of the other words in this class are listed below.

| नातू | natu | grandson |
| पू | pu | pus |
| लाडू | laḍu | a ball–shaped sweet |
| विंचू | vincu | scorpion |

( d ) Ending in a consonant

( i ) There is no difference between the straight singular and the straight plural.

| एक हात | ek hat | one hand |
| दोन हात | don hat | two hands |

( ii ) The oblique singular and plural are formed according to the rule: + *a*.

| एका हातात | eka hatat | in one hand |
| दोन हातांत | don hatat | in two hands |

---

* According to the rule this becomes *gəhva*, but the *v* is actually pronounced first.

( e ) Ending in *o*

> We have encountered only two words in this class. They do not
> undergo any change in the plural or the oblique.

| | | |
|---|---|---|
| धनको | dhənko | creditor |
| पो | po | small heap of dung |

## ( 2 ) Neuter

### (a) Marked

( i ) The straight plural is formed according to the rule: ə : → *i*.

| | | |
|---|---|---|
| भांडं | bhaṇḍə: | vessel |
| भांडी | bhaṇḍi | vessels |

( ii ) The oblique singular and plural are formed according to
the rule:

ə: → *ya*.

| | | |
|---|---|---|
| एका भांड्यात | eka bhaṇḍyat | in one vessel |
| दोन भांड्यांत | don bhaṇḍyat | in two vessels |

### (b) Ending in *u*.

Class 1.

( i ) The straight plural is formed according to the rule: *u* → ə:.
In formal speech and writing the rule is: u → *e*.

| | | |
|---|---|---|
| पिल्लू | pillu | young of an animal |
| पिल्लं | pillə: | young of an animal ( pl. ) |
| लिंबू | limbu | lemon |
| लिंबं | limbə: | lemons |

( ii ) The oblique singular and plural are formed according to the
rule: *u* → *a*.

| | | |
|---|---|---|
| पिल्लू | pillu | young of an animal |
| पिल्लाला | pillala | to the young of an animal |
| पिल्लांना | pillanna | to the young animals |
| लिंबू | limbu | lemon |
| लिंबाला | limbala | for the lemon |
| लिंबांना | limbanna | for the lemons |

Other words in this class include the following.

| पाखरू | pakhru | bird |
|-------|--------|------|
| रेडकू | reḍku | young buffalo |
| मेंढरू | meṇḍhru | sheep |
| वासरू | vasru | calf |
| शिंगरू | šiŋgru | colt |
| कोकरू | kokru | lamb |
| तट्टू | təṭṭu | pony |
| करडू | kərḍu | kid |

## Class 2

(iii) The straight plural is formed by the rule: $+ \partial{:}$ with application of Rule $M_2$.

| गळू | gəḷu | boil |
|-----|------|------|
| गळवं | gəḷvə: | boils |

(iv) The oblique singular and plural are formed according to the rule: $u \to a$, with application of Rule $M_2$.

| गळवात | gəḷvat | in the boil |
|--------|--------|-------------|
| गळवांत | gəḷvat | in the boils |

Other words in this class include the following.

| कुंकू | kuŋku | vermillion powder |
|-------|-------|-------------------|
| गू | gu | human excrement |

## ( c ) Ending in *i*

( i ) Neuter nouns ending in *i* are all uncountable nouns, so they have no plural forms.*

( ii ) The oblique singular is formed according to the rule: $+ a$, with application of Rule $M_1$.

| पाणी | paṇi | water |
|------|------|-------|
| पाण्यात | paṇyat | in the water |
| दही | dəhi | curds |
| दह्यात | dəhyat | in the curds |

*The one exception is *moti* ' pearl. ' However, this is treated as masculine by some speakers and all speakers use the masculine form *moti* for the plural.

( d ) Ending in a consonant

( i ) The straight plural is formed according to the rule: + ə:. In formal speech and in writing the rule is: + e.

| घर | ghər | house |
| घरं | ghərə: | houses |

( ii ) The oblique singular and plural are formed according to the rule: + a.

| घर | ghər | house |
| घरात | ghərat | in the house |
| घरांत | ghərat | in the houses |

(iii) The words *paul* ' foot ' and *deuḷ* ' temple ' follow the regular rules for formation of plural and oblique forms. In addition, however, the medial *u* is changed to *v*.

| पावलं | pavlə: | feet |
| पावलात | pavḷat | in the fooi |
| पावलांत | pavḷat | in the feet |
| देवळं | devḷə: | temples |
| देवळात | devḷat | in the temple |
| देवळांत | devḷat | in the temples |

( iv ) The oblique singular of *pitəḷ* ' brass ' is *pitəḷe—*.

( 3 ) **Feminine**

( a ) Marked

Class 1

( i ) The straight singular and the oblique singular are the same.

| गाडी | gaḍi | car |
| गाडीनी | gaḍini | by car |
| पेटी | peṭi | box |
| पेटीत | peṭit | in the box |

( ii ) The straight and oblique plural are formed according to the rule: + a, with application of Rule M₁.

| गाडी | gaḍi | car |
| गाड्या | gaḍya | cars |
| गाड्यांनी | gaḍyanni | by the cars |

| पेटी | peṭi | box |
| पेट्या | peṭya | boxes |
| पेट्यांत | peṭyat | in the boxes |

## Class 2

( iii ) There is a set of feminine nouns ending in *i* which undergo no change in the plural, straight or oblique. Some of the nouns in this set are listed below. Note that they are all borrowings from Sanskrit.

| देवी | devi | goddess |
| तरुणी | tǝruṇi | young woman |
| गृहिणी | grihiṇi | housewife |
| वृत्ती | vrɪtti | attitude |
| प्रवृत्ती | prǝvritti | tendency |
| आवृत्ती | avritti | edition |
| पद्धती | pǝddhǝti | system |
| आकृती | akrɪti | form, figure, shape |
| उक्ती | ukti | utterance |
| आपत्ती | apǝtti | calamity |
| अस्थी | ǝsthi | bone |

( iv ) The straight plural and oblique singular and plural of *mulgi* is *muli*. Similarly *porgi* ' girl ' ( C ) becomes *pori*.

| मुलगी | mulgi | girl |
| मुली | muli | girls |
| | | |
| मुलीला | mulila | to the girl |
| मुलींना | mulinna | to the girls |

( v ) The straight and oblique plural of *bai* is normally *bayka*, although the regular form *baya* is also used.

| बाई | bai | woman |
| बायका, बाया | bayka, baya | women |

When *bai* is used to mean ' woman ' it is treated as singular. When it is used as a respectful form it is treated as plural.

| एक बाई आली आहे. | ek bai ali ae. |
| | A woman has come. |

सीताबाई आल्या आहेत.                    Sitabai alya aet.

Sitabai has come.

When *bai* is used as a respectful form an *anusvar* is required in the oblique.

सीताबाईंना हे द्या.                      Sitabainna he dya.

Give this to Sitabai.

Note that this form is different from the oblique plural.

बायकांना ( बायांना ) हे द्या.            baykanna (bayanna) he dya.

Give this to the women.

( b ) Ending in *u*

Class 1

( i ) For this class there is no change either for the oblique singular or for the straight and oblique plural.

| एक वस्तू | ek vəstu | one object |
| एका वस्तूला | eka vəstula | for one object |
| दोन वस्तू | don vəstu | two objects |
| दोन वस्तूंना | don vəstunna | for two objects |

Other nouns in this set include the following.

| वधू | vədhu | bride |
| डाळू | taḷu | crown of head |

Class 2

( ii ) The straight and oblique plural is formed according to the rule: + *a*, with application of Rule M$_2$.

| सासू | sasu | mother–in–law |
| सासवा | sasva | mothers–in–law |
| सासवांना | sasvanna | to the mothers–in–law |
| जाऊ | jau | sister–in–law |
| जावा | java | sisters–in–law |
| जावांना | javanna | to the sisters–in–law |

Other nouns in this set include the following.

| जळू | jəḷu | leech |
| पिसू | pisu | flea |
| ऊ | u | louse |

( iii ) For all the above words except *u* the oblique singular may be formed according to the rule: + *e* with application of Rule M$_2$.

| सासवेला | sasvela | to the mother–in–law |
| जावेला | javela | to the sister–in–law |
| जळवेला | jəlvela | to the leech |
| पिसवेला | pisvela | to the flea |

For all these words except *jau* the straight singular may be used without change for the oblique singular. This form, in fact, is more common today.

| सासूला | sasula | to the mother–in–law |

## ( c ) Ending in *a*

( i ) The oblique singular is formed according to the rule: *a* → *e*.

| शाळा | šaḷa | school |
| शाळेत | šaḷet | in the school |
| पूजा | puja | (ritual) worship |
| पूजेत | pujet | in the worship |

( ii ) The straight and oblique plurals are the same as the straight singular.

| एक शाळा | ek šaḷa | one school |
| दोन शाळा | don šaḷa | two schools |
| दोन शाळांत | don šaḷat | in two schools |

## ( d ) Ending in a consonant

Feminine nouns ending in a consonant fall into two groups, depending on how their oblique singular is formed.

( i ) Some nouns, which we shall refer to as *f.(e)*, form the oblique singular according to the rule: + *e*.

| खेप | khep | turn |
| खेपेला | khepela | on the turn |
| सून | sun | daughter-in-law |
| सुनेला | sunela | to the daughter-in-law |

( ii ) The straight and oblique plural of *f.(e)* nouns is formed according to the rule: + *a*.

| खेप | khep | turn |
| खेपा | khepa | turns |
| खेपांना | khepanna | on the turns |
| सून | sun | daughter-in-law |
| सुना | suna | daughters-in-law |
| सुनांना | sunanna | to the daughters-in-law |

( iii ) Other nouns, which we shall refer to as *f.(i)*, form the singular oblique and straight and oblique plural according to the rule: + *i*.

| बहीण | bəhiṇ | sister |
| बहिणीला | bəhiṇila | to the sister |
| बहिणी | bəhiṇi | sisters |
| बहिर्णीना | bəhiṇinna | to the sisters |

(iv) There are a number of nouns which form the oblique singular according to the *f.(i)* class but the straight and oblique plural according to the *f.(e)* class.

| चूक | cuk | mistake |
| चुकीला | cukila | for the mistake |
| चुका | cuka | mistakes |
| चुकांना | cukanna | for the mistakes |

Other nouns in this set include the following.

| टप्पल | ṭəppəl | slap |
| थप्पड | thəpped̪ | slap |

( e ) Ending in *o*

We have encountered only one feminine noun ending in *o*. This is *bayko* ' wife. ' The oblique singular remains unchanged. The straight and oblique plural is *bayka*.

The rules for formation of plural and oblique noun forms are summarized in Table 3.1.

Table 3.1.     *Rules for Formation of Plural and Oblique Noun Forms*

| Masculine | Str. Pl. | Obl. Sing. and Pl. |
|---|---|---|
| Marked ( ending in *a* ) | | |
|     Class 1 | a → e | a → ya |
|     Class 2 | ya → e | no change |
| Ending in *i* | | |
|     Class 1 | no change | + a ( with $M_1$ ) |
|     Class 2 | no change | no change |
| Ending in *u* | | |
|     Class 1 | no change | no change |
|     Class 2 | no change | + a ( with $M_2$ ) |
| Ending in consonant | no change | + a |
| Ending in *o* | no change | no change |

| Neuter | Str. Pl. | Obl. Sing. and Pl. |
|---|---|---|
| Marked ( ending in ə: ) | ə: → i | ə: → ya |
| Ending in *u* | | |
|     Class 1 | u → ə: | u → a |
|     Class 2 | + ə: ( with $M_2$ ) | + a ( with $M_2$ ) |
| Ending in *i* | — | + a ( with $M_1$ ) |
| Ending in consonant | ə: | + a |

| Feminine | Obl. Sing. | Str. and Obl. Pl. |
|---|---|---|
| Marked ( ending in *i* ) | | |
|     Class 1 | no change | + a ( with $M_1$ ) |
|     Class 2 | no change | no change |
| Ending in *u* | | |
|     Class 1 | no change | no change |
|     Class 2 | + e ( with $M_2$ ) | + a ( with $M_2$ ) |
| Ending in *a* | a → e | no change |
| Ending in consonant | | |
|     Class f. (e) | + e | + a |
|     Class f (i) | + i | + i |
| Ending in *o* | no change | o → a |

General rule: When an oblique plural is followed by a postposition beginning with a consonant, a nasal of the same articulatory series is inserted before the postposition.

### 3. Other morphophonemic rules

In addition to the rules already discussed there are several other morphophonemic rules affecting nouns of any gender ending in a consonant. It should be noted that Rules $M_6$, $M_{7i}$, $M_{7ii}$, and $M_9$ automatically follow from the general rule that *i* and *u* in non-final syllables are short.

(1) Rule $M_5$

*c j, jh* and *s* become respectively *č, ǰ, jȟ*, and *š* before the addition of or *y*, and, optionally, before the addition of *e*.

| भाचा | bhaca | nephew |
| भाच्याला | bhačyala | to the nephew |
| घसा | ghəsa | throat |
| घश्यात | ghəšyat | in the throat |
| लस | ləs | vaccine |
| लशी | ləši | vaccines |

(2) Rule $M_6$

In a one-syllable word consisting of the sequence $CV_wC$ where $V_w$ is the vowel *i* or *u*, the vowel is shortened before the addition of another vowel.

| मीठ | mĭṭh | salt |
| मिठात | mĭṭhat | in the salt |
| दूध | dūdh | milk |
| दुधात | dŭdhat | in the milk |
| मूळ | mūl | child |
| मुळं | mŭlə: | children |
| फीत | phĭt | ribbon |
| फिती | phĭti | ribbons |
| टीप | ṭĭp | note |
| टिपेला | ṭĭpela | to the note |

(3) Rule $M_7$

In a word of two or more syllables ending in the sequence $V_wCV_wC$, if the second vowel is *ə*, *i*, or *u* it is deleted before the addition of a vowel. This deletion is not always indicated in writing.

* $V_w$ = Vowel

| कागद | kagəd | paper |
| कागदावर | kagdavər | on the paper |
| वडील | vəḍil | father |
| वडिलांना | vəḍlanna | to the fathers, to |
| ( वडलांना ) | | father, (*respect.*) |
| साखर | sakhər | sugar |
| साखरेत | sakhret | in the sugar |
| लसूण | ləsuṇ | garlic |
| लसणाचं | ləsṇacə: | of garlic |

There are many exceptions to this rule, and it is difficult to formulate any generalization to account for the exceptions. However, the following rough guidelines may be used.

( a ) If the medial consonant is *h*, the following vowel is not dropped, but in the case of *i* and *u* it is shortened.

| शहर | šəhər | city |
| शहरात | šəhərat | in the city |
| बहीण | bəhĭṇ | sister |
| बहिणीला | bəhĭṇila | to the sister |

( b ) In borrowings from other languages the vowel is not dropped, but in the case of *i* and *u* it is shortened.

| वजीर | vəjĭr | prime minister |
| बजिराला | vəjĭrala | to the prime minister |

( c ) In borrowings from Sanskrit the vowel is generally not dropped, but in the case of *i* and *u* it is often shortened. However, according to the current rules of *šuddhəlekhən* ( correct writing ) these vowels are supposed to be written long.

| शरीर | šərĭr | body |
| शरीरात | šərĭrat | in the body |
| स्वरूप | svərūp | form |
| स्वरूपात | svərŭpat | in the form |

( 4 ) Rule $M_8$

In words of two or more syllables ending in the sequence $V_w C_1 C_1 V_w C_2$

where $C_1C_1$ is a double consonant, the double consonant is made single
and the second vowel is deleted before the addition of a vowel.

| गम्मत | gəmmət | fun |
| गमतीचं | gəmticə: | of fun |
| रक्कम | rəkkəm | amount |
| रकमा | rəkma | amounts |

(5) Rule $M_9$

In words of two or more syllables ending in the sequence $V_wC_1C_2V_wC$,
where $C_1C_2$ is a conjunct consonant, if the second vowel is *i* or *u* it
is shortened before the addition of a vowel.

| मैत्रीण | məitrin̥ | friend |
| मैत्रिणी | məitrin̥i | friends |

## 4. Locative

The preceding discussion accounts for the majority of the noun forms usually
encountered. However, there are a few forms which are vestiges of an older
grammatical system. One of these is the locative, which functions as an adverb.
It is formed by adding *i* directly to the noun without a change to the oblique
form. The locative can be used only with certain nouns. Some of the most
common of these are listed below.

| घर | ghər | house |
| घरी | ghəri | in the house |
| पाय | pay | foot |
| पायी | payi | on foot |
| दिवस | divəs | day |
| दिवशी | divši* | on (the) day |

## 5. Vocative

The vocative, a special form for address, is going out of use, but is still
encountered occasionally. It is obviously used mainly in addressing people, though
it may be employed for addressing a creature or inanimate object that one

* Note the operation of Rules $M_5$ and $M_7$.

wants to personify. For the vocative singular, the bare oblique singular form is used. For the vocative plural, the oblique plural form with the ending *no* is used. In the examples below the first word in each set is the straight form; the second is the vocative.

| | | |
|---|---|---|
| मूल | mul | child |
| मुला | mula* | |
| मुलं | mulə: | children |
| मुलांनो | mulanno | |
| मुलगी | mulgi | girl |
| मुली | muli | |
| मुली | muli | girls |
| मुलींनो | mulinno | |

## B.  Adjectives

Classified by form, adjectives are of two types: variable and invariable. Invariable adjectives do not undergo any change in form. Variable adjectives must agree in gender and number with the nouns they modify.

## 1.  Variable adjectives

The variable adjective endings are listed below, followed by examples.

| Singular | | | Plural | | |
|---|---|---|---|---|---|
| M | F | N | M | F | N |
| a | i | ə:** | e | ya | i |

| | | |
|---|---|---|
| चांगला रस्ता | caŋgla rəsta | good road |
| चांगली गाडी | caŋgli gaḍi | good car |
| चांगलं पुस्तक | caŋglə: pustək | good book |
| चांगले रस्ते | caŋgle rəste | good roads |
| चांगल्या गाड्या | caŋglya gaḍya | good cars |
| चांगली पुस्तकं | caŋgli pustəkə: | good books |

*Note the operation of Rule M₆ throughout this list.

**As elsewhere, the written form is *e* and the spoken form is ə:.

2.  Invariable adjectives

| लांब रस्ता | lamb rəsta | long road |
| लहान गाडी | ləhan gaḍi | little car |
| लहान पुस्तक | ləhan pustək | little book |
| लांब रस्ते | lamb rəste | long roads |
| लहान गाड्या | ləhan gaḍya | little cars |
| लहान पुस्तकं | ləhan pustəkə: | little books |

**Oblique form.** A variable adjective modifying a noun in the oblique must also be in the oblique. The oblique is formed by changing the adjective ending to *ya*.

| चांगला रस्ता | caŋgla rəsta | good road |
| चांगल्या रस्त्यावर | caŋglya rəstyavər | on a good road |
| मोठी गाडी | moṭhi gaḍi | big car |
| मोठ्या गाडीनी | moṭhya gaḍini | with a big car |

There may be several adjectives modifying a noun in the oblique. In this case all the adjectives must be in the oblique.

माझ्या थोरल्या भावाची मुलगी      majhya thorlya bhavači mulgi
                                 my elder brother's daughter

## C.  Pronouns

### 1. Subject pronouns

The Marathi pronoun system has several complications unfamiliar to English speakers. As correct pronoun use is bound up with the etiquette of the language, the student must take care to master the forms and their uses.

**First Person.** The first person forms are the least complicated. The first person singular ( Eng. ' I ' ) is *mi.** In using the plural ( Eng. ' we ' ), however, the speaker must make it clear whether or not the pronoun includes the person spoken to. The inclusive ' we ' is *apən*; the exclusive, *amhi*.

*Some people occasionally refer to themselves ( singly ) as *amhi*, but this is generally considered bad form.

**Second Person.** For directly addressing a person, the selection of pronouns depends on the speaker's social relationship to that person. There are three levels of social distance and respect. The corresponding pronouns are:

| | | |
|---|---|---|
| ( a ) Familiar | तू | tu |
| ( b ) Respectful | तुम्ही | tumhi |
| ( c ) Honorific | आपण | apən |

The honorific form *apən* indicates the greatest degree of social distance and respect. In everyday conversation the use of *apən* is decreasing. Often people who are introduced will use it in their first meeting, then switch to *tumhi* in subsequent meetings. Generally, continued use of *apən* is reserved for those to whom one wants to show special deference.<sup>*</sup>

If the social relationship does not call for the use of the honorific, the speaker must still choose between the familiar and the respectful. There are complications in the principles underlying the selection of these forms, but the most essential rules are given below.

( a ) The familiar is used for children, close friends, siblings, mother, mother's sister, and grandmother.

( b ) For all others the respectful is used. Note that this includes father and husband.

( c ) Some people address servants in the familiar, but a foreigner would be better advised to use the respectful. In fact, the general rule is: *When in doubt, use the respectful.*

The discussion above relates to pronoun choice when the speaker is speaking to one person. In speaking to a group he has only to choose between the respectful and the honorific. The honorific is used only for formal situations; otherwise, the respectful is used.**

---

<sup>*</sup>It sometimes happens that people are extra polite to foreigners, and a young foreigner may find himself being addressed as *apən* by an elderly person. In this case the younger person must continue to use *apən*, at least until the elder shifts to *tumhi*.

<sup>*</sup>From this sketch it should be clear that respectful forms are plural forms. The identification of plurality and respect is quite common, not only in Indian languages but in European languages as well. In fact, English ' you ' was originally a plural / respectful form. The old singular / familiar form ' thou ' has dropped out of use. For a further discussion of the use of respectful forms, see Appendix B.

**Third Person.** The third person may be used to refer to objects, ideas, creatures, or people. In referring to any of the first three categories. the choice of pronoun depends upon two factors:

( a ) the gender and number of the noun for which the pronoun is a replacement.

( b ) the proximity of the object in question. ( Cf. Eng. ' this, that, ' )

The pronouns used to refer to objects, creatures or ideas are listed in Table 3.2.

Table 3.2.     *Third Person Non-Personal Pronoun Forms*

|  | Singular | | | Plural | | |
|---|---|---|---|---|---|---|
|  | M | F | N | M | F | N |
| Distant | तो | ती | ते | ते | त्या | ती |
|  | to | ti | te | te | tya | ti |
| Proximate | हा | ही | हे | हे | ह्या | ही |
|  | ha | hi | he | he | hya* | hi |

In referring to a person in the third person, a speaker's choice of pronoun depends upon three factors:

( a ) the sex of the person spoken of
( b ) the social distance between the speaker and the person spoken of
( c ) the proximity of the person spoken of

In the third person there are only two degrees of respect: familiar and respect-ful; there is no special honorific form.  For the familiar the set of pronouns is the same as for non-personal nouns. See the singular forms listed in Table 3.2 above.

Reference to a person in the neuter singular is not common, but may occur n referring to a child, either because the sex is not evident or important, or as

*In speech *hya* is often replaced by *ya*. 1n writing also या is sometimes used.

an expression of contempt. In the latter case, the neuter is used only for a boy.

For respectful reference in the third person the speaker uses the masculine or feminine plural forms. The third person respectful forms are listed in Table 3.3.

Table 3.3.  *Third Person Respectful Forms*

|  | M | F |
|---|---|---|
| Distant | ते<br>te | त्या<br>tya |
|  | M | F |
| Proximate | हे<br>he | ह्या<br>hya |

In the third person plural the question of respectful forms does not arise, so the only factors governing the selection of pronouns are the sex and proximity of the person referred to. The third person plural personal pronouns are the same as the non–personal plural pronouns listed above in Table 3.2.

Unlike the singular, the third person plural neuter pronouns are frequently used to refer to people. They are used either for a mixed group of men and women or boys and girls, or for a group of men or boys. For a group of women or girls the feminine will be used.

The pronouns discussed above are summarized in Table 3.4.

Table 3.4.    *Subject Pronouns*

**First person**

| | | |
|---|---|---|
| मी | mi | I |
| आम्ही | amhi | we ( *excl.* ) |
| आपण | apəṇ | we ( *incl.* ) |

**Second person**

| | | |
|---|---|---|
| तू | tu | you ( *fam. sg.* ) |
| तुम्ही | tumhi | you ( *respect., pl.* ) |
| आपण | apəṇ | you ( *hon.* ) |

**Third person**

**Distant**

| | | |
|---|---|---|
| तो | to | he ( *fam.* ), it ( *m.* ) |
| ती | ti | she ( *fam.* ), it ( *f.* ) |
| ते | te | it ( *n.* ) |
| ते | te | he ( *respect.* ), they ( *m.* ) |
| त्या | tya | she ( *respect.* ), they ( *f.* ) |
| ती | ti | they ( *n.* ) |

**Proximate**

| | | |
|---|---|---|
| हा | ha | he ( *fam.* ), it ( *m.* ) |
| ही | hi | she ( *fam.* ), it ( *m.* ) |
| हे | he | it ( *n.* ) |
| हे | he | he ( *respect.* ), they ( *m.* ) |
| ह्या | hya | she ( *respect.* ), they ( *f.* ) |
| ही | hi | they ( *n.* ) |

## 2. Object pronouns

If a pronoun refers to a non–personal noun, it may be used as a direct object. The direct object pronoun has the same form as the subject pronoun. For instance, the sentence ' I do that ' may have three possible forms, depending on the gender of the noun referred to.

| | |
|---|---|
| मी तो करतो. | mi to kərto. |
| मी ती करतो. | mi ti kərto. |
| मी ते करतो. | mi te kərto. |

A pronoun referring to a person may not generally be used as a direct object. The postposition *la* or *na* must be added to the pronoun, making it indirect. Before *la* or *na* special form of the pronouns are required. These are listed in Table 3.5. Note that *la* is used with singular pronouns and *na* with plural. Note also that in the singular *to* and *te* both become *tyala*, and *ha* and *he* both become *hyala*. Similarly, in the plural *te*, *tye* and *ti* all become *tyanna*, and *he*, *hya* and *hi* all become *hyanna*.

In English these forms will be translated either as direct objects or as indirect objects, depending on the context of the sentence, as illustrated in the examples below.

मी त्याला ओळखतो.          mi tyala oḷəkhto.
                          I know him.

मी त्याला लिहितो.          mi tyala lihito.
                          I write to him.

*Table 3.5.*      *Indirect Object Pronoun Forms*

| Subject form | | Indirect object form | |
|---|---|---|---|
| मी | mi | मला | məla |
| तू | tu | तुला | tula* |
| तो, ते | to, te ( *sg.* ) | त्याला | tyala |
| ती | ti ( *sg.* ) | तिला | tila |
| हा, हे | ha, he ( *sg.* ) | ह्याला | hyala |
| ही | hi | हिला | hila |
| आम्ही | amhi | आम्हाला | amhala |
| तुम्ही | tumhi | तुम्हाला | tumhala |
| ते, त्या, ती | te, tya, ti ( *pl.* ) | त्यांना | tyanna |
| हे, ह्या, ही | he, hya, hi ( *pl.* ) | ह्यांना | hyanna |
| आपण | apəṇ | आपल्याला | aplyala |

## 3. Possessives

The possessive pronouns consist of a special possessive stem plus the regular adjective endings, agreeing in gender and number with the noun they modify.

*Note the operation of Rule $M_6$ throughout the table.

Since these have the form and function of adjectives they will be referred to in this text as possessive adjectives. The possessive adjectives are listed in Table 3.6 below.

Table 3.6.        *Possessive Adjectives*

| M | F | N | M | F | N |
|---|---|---|---|---|---|
| माझा | माझी | माझं | माझे | माइया | माझी |
| majha | maǰhi* | majhə:** | majhe | maǰhya | majhi |
| तुझा | तुझी | तुझं | तुझे | तुइया | तुझी |
| tujha** | tuǰhi | tujhə: | tujhe | tuǰhya | tuǰhi |
| त्याचा | त्याची | त्याचं | त्याचे | त्याच्या | त्याची |
| tyaca | tyači | tyacə: | tyace | tyačya | tyači |
| ह्याचा | ह्याची | ह्याचं | ह्याचे | ह्याच्या | ह्याची |
| hyaca | hyači | hyacə: | hyace | hyačya | hyači |
| तिचा | तिची | तिचं | तिचे | तिच्या | तिची |
| tica | tiči | ticə: | tice | tičya | tiči |
| हिचा | हिची | हिचं | हिचे | हिच्या | हिची |
| hica | hiči | hicə: | hice | hičya | hiči |
| आमचा | आमची | आमचं | आमचे | आमच्या | आमची |
| amca | amči | amcə: | amce | amčya | amči |
| तुमचा | तुमची | तुमचं | तुमचे | तुमच्या | तुमची |
| tumca | tumči | tumcə: | tumce | tumčya | tumči |
| त्यांचा | त्यांची | त्यांचं | त्यांचे | त्यांच्या | त्यांची |
| tyanca | tyanči | tyancə: | tyance | tyančya | tyanči |
| ह्यांचा | ह्यांची | ह्यांचं | ह्यांचे | ह्यांच्या | ह्यांची |
| hyanca | hyanči | hyancə: | hyance | hyančya | hyanči |
| आपळा | आपळी | आपळं | आपळे | आपळ्या | आपळी |
| apla | apli | aplə: | aple | aplya | apli |

\* Note the operation of Rule $M_5$ throughout the table.

\*\*As with other adjectives, the written form of the n. sg. ending is *e*.

\*\*\*Note the operation of Rule $M_6$ throughout the table.

## 4. Pronoun + *ni*

In certain constructions a pronoun is to be combined with the instrumental postposition *ni.*[*] In this case special forms of the pronoun are required. These forms are listed in Table 3.7. They may be translated literally as ' by me, ' ' by you, ' etc., but the corresponding English sentences will normally have the pronouns in the subject form, i. e., ' I, ' ' you, ' etc.

Table 3.7.    *Forms of Pronouns Used with ni*

| Subject form | | Form with *ni* | |
|---|---|---|---|
| मी | mi | मी | mi |
| तू | tu | तू | tu |
| तो, ते | to, te ( *sg.* ) | त्यानी | tyani |
| ती | ti ( *sg.* ) | तिनी | tini** |
| हा, हे | ha, he ( *sg.* ) | ह्यानी | hyani |
| ही | hi | हिनी | hini |
| आम्ही | amhi | आम्ही | amhi |
| तुम्ही | tumhi | तुम्ही | tumhi |
| ते, त्या, ती | te, tya, ti ( *pl.* ) | त्यांनी | tyanni |
| हे, ह्या, ही | he, hya, hi ( *pl.* ) | ह्यांनी | hyanni |
| आपण | apǝṇ | आपण | apǝṇ |

Note that only the third person pronouns have special forms. In the other persons the *ni* is theoretically there but is not actually present.

## 5. Oblique form of pronouns

Before postpositions other than *la* ( *na* ) and *ni,* pronouns must be in the oblique form. For pronouns referring to persons the possessive is used as the base for the oblique. For masculine and neuter pronouns referring to non-personal nouns the subject form is often used as the base. Whichever base is used, the rule for the ending is the same: the ending is changed to *ya.*[***]

---

[*]The form *ni* is used in speech; *ne* is used in writing. Some speakers use *nǝ:*, instead of *ni* as the spoken form.

[**]Note application of Rule $M_6$ throughout the table.

[***]Sometimes the neuter singular form of the pronoun is used as the oblique but this is considered incorrect.

( 1 ) Examples of pronouns referring to persons

| | | |
|---|---|---|
| माझं | majhə: | my |
| माझ्याजवळ | ma͡jhyajəvəḷ* | near me |
| त्याचं | tyacə: | his |
| त्याच्यासाठी | tyačyasaṭhi | for him |
| तुमचं | tumcə: | your |
| तुमच्याकडे | tumčyakəḍe | to your place, to you |
| आमचं | amcə: | our |
| आमच्याकडून | amčyakəḍun | from us |

( 2 ) Examples of pronouns referring to non–personal nouns

| | | |
|---|---|---|
| ते | te | that |
| त्यानंतर | tyanəntər | after that |
| त्यामुळे | tyamuḷe | because of that |
| त्यात | tyat | in that |
| त्यांत | tyat | in those |
| त्यांच्यात | tyančyat | in those |
| ती | ti (*f.*) | that |
| तिच्यात | tičyat | in that |
| त्यांच्यात | tyančyat | in those |

## 6. Demonstrative adjectives

The demonstrative adjectives are pronouns used with a following noun.

| | | |
|---|---|---|
| तो माणूस | to maṇus | that man |
| हा माणूस | ha maṇus | this man |
| ती गाय | ti gay | that cow |
| ही गाय | hi gay | this cow |
| ते घर | te ghər | that house |
| हे घर | he ghər | this house |
| आम्ही लोक | amhi lok | we people |
| तुम्ही लोक | tumhi lok | you people |

*Note the operation of Rule M₅ throughout the list.

## 7. Oblique form of demonstrative and possessive adjectives

When the noun they are modifying is in the oblique, demonstrative and possessive adjectives must also be in the oblique. The oblique form of *amhi* is *amha* and the oblique form of *tumhi* is *tumha*. For all other demonstratives and possessive adjectives the ending is *ya*, regardless of the gender or number of the noun modified.

| | | |
|---|---|---|
| माझा भाऊ | majha bhau | my brother |
| माझ्या भावाला | majhya bhavala | to my brother |
| | | |
| त्याची मुलं | tyačì mulə: | his children |
| त्याच्या मुलांकडून | tyačya mulaŋkədun | from his children |
| | | |
| तो मुलगा | to mulga | that boy |
| त्या मुलाला | tya mulala | to that boy |
| | | |
| ते गाव | te gav | that town |
| त्या गावाला | tya gavala | to that town |
| | | |
| ती गाडी | ti gaḍi | that car |
| त्या गाडीत | tya gaḍit | in that car |
| | | |
| आम्ही लोक | amhi lok | we people |
| आम्हा लोकांना | amha lokanna | to us ( people ) |

## 8. Reflexive pronouns

The pronoun *apən*, which has already been introduced, also functions as a reflexive pronoun. It is used when there is a second reference to the subject within a sentence, e.g.:

| | |
|---|---|
| ते आपल्या मुलांना शाळेत पाठवत नाहीत. | te aplya mulanna šaḷet paṭhvət nahit. |
| | They do not send their children to school. |
| त्याला असं वाटलं की आपण ते काम करावं. | tyala əsə: vatlə: ki apən te kam kəravə:, |
| | He felt that he should do the work. |

आपला भाऊ सहस्रभोजन घालतो
आहे.

apla bhau səhəsrəbhojən ghalto
ae.

My brother is giving a great feast
for Brahmans.

In some cases *apəṇ* serves to qualify the subject, somewhat as the phrases
' at least, ' ' for one, ' and ' on his part' do in English.

मी आपला जाणार आहे.

mi apla jaṇar ae.*
I for one am going to go.

ती आपली तशीच जेवली.

ti apli təšic jevli.
She ( on her part ) ate her meal.

The other reflexive pronoun is *svətəhə*.

तो स्वतःशी बोलतो.

to svətəhəši bolto.
He talks to himself.

तो स्वतःला मोठा समजतो.

to svətəhəla moṭha səməjto.
He considers himself important.

तिनी स्वतः काम केलं.

tini svətəhə kam kelə:.
She did the work herself.

## D.   Interrogative Forms

Nouns, pronouns, and adjectives may be replaced  by interrogatives  to  form
questions. Following are the interrogative forms.

| Straight form | | Oblique form | | |
|---|---|---|---|---|
| काय | kay | कशा | kəša– | what |
| कोण | koṇ | कोणा | koṇa– | who |
| कोणतं | koṇtə: ( var. ) | कोणत्या | koṇtya | which |

*Note that in this sentence and the one following, *aplə*: is  a  variable  adjective
agreeing with the subject in gender and number.

# Chapter four

# VERBS

## A. Classification

### 1. Transitive–intransitive

Marathi verbs can be classified in two principal ways. First, according to whether or not they take a direct object, verbs are classified as *transitive* or *intransitive*. Transitive verbs are those that take a direct object; intransitive verbs are those that do not. Transitive verbs are further divided according to the agreement rules they follow for the formation of the perfect construction. The majority of transitive verbs are referred to in this text simply as transitive verbs, *v.t.* A special sub–class is referred to as special transitive verbs, *v.t. (sp.)*. Intransitive verbs are referred to as *v.i.*

### 2. Personal–impersonal

Verbs may also be classified according to whether or not they can have a personal noun as subject. Those which can are called *personal verbs*; those which cannot are *impersonal verbs*. (It should be kept in mind, however, that this distinction is not always clear-cut.) For the most part, verbs which are impersonal in Marathi are impersonal in English also, and they present no special difficulty. Below are some examples of impersonal verbs. Note that they are all intransitive.

| | | |
|---|---|---|
| ताप– | tap– | to heat |
| निव– | niv– | to cool |
| शिज– | šij– | to cook |
| गळ– | gəḷ– | to drip |
| संप– | səmp– | to finish, be used up |
| वाळ– | vaḷ– | to dry |

There is a subset of impersonal verbs that cause special problems to the student whose mother–tongue is English. Many of these verbs deal with desire, perception, or feeling. In English such verbs have personal subjects, as in the sentences below.

> I like ice cream.
> My sister wants this book.
> My brother doesn't feel well.

In the corresponding Marathi sentences the person is the object, not the subject.

मला आइस्क्रिम आवडतं.

maəla ayskrim avədtə:.
I like ice cream.
( Lit., ' ice cream pleases me. ' )

माझ्या बहिणीला हे पुस्तक पाहिजे.

majhya bəhiṇila he pustək pahije.
My sister wants this book.
( Lit., ' to my sister this book is required. ' )

माझ्या भावाला बरं वाटत नाही.

majhya bhavala bərə: vaʈət nahi.
My brother doen't feel well.
( Lit., ' to my brother it does not feel well. ' )

( The " literal " translations above are, of course, very awkward. They are given merely to convey an idea of how the Marathi sentence is constructed. ) These verbs will be referred to as *N–la impersonal verbs*.

## 3. Tense and aspect

Students are accustomed to thinking about verbs in terms of tense — usually divided into present, past, and future. Even for English these categories are not really accurate, and for Marathi they are definitely not. To understand the Marathi verbal system it is necessary to grasp the difference between two key concepts — tense and aspect.

Tense refers to the location of an action in time. The time sequence is often divided into past, present, and future, but it should be kept in mind that these categories are relative and their meaning shifts according to context. In one context the present may be the present moment and the past a minute earlier. In other contexts the present may be a day, a year, a century, or even a geological era. That is, our time scale can expand or contract according to our communicative needs.

Aspect, on the other hand, refers not to the time of occurrence of an action but to the way it is viewed. This is not an easy concept to grasp but it is perhaps understandable if we think of the various ways a movie camera can show an action — a horse jumping over a fence, for example. One possibility is showing the action in slow motion, so that we see the animal gradually rise and fall, see the changing degrees of tension in his muscles. Another possibility is showing the action at normal speed, so the viewer sees it as a complete unit. A third possibility is showing a series of pictures of the same action to suggest repetition. In aspect we have the verbal equivalent of the cameraman's technique. A verbal construction combining information about both aspect and tense enables the speaker to convey the exact nuances he wants to emphasize in regard to a particular action.

## 4. Tense in Marathi

In Marathi only the verb *əs*– ' to be ' has a full range of tenses: past, present, future, and habitual. The past and present have the meanings one would expect, but the future has an unexpected element. It may convey pure futurity or may simply indicate probability. The habitual is used for habitual action in the past.

## 5. Aspect in Marathi

Marathi has three aspects — perfect, imperfect, and prospective. In the perfect, action is viewed as complete. In the imperfect, action is either viewed as in progress or habitual. In the prospective, action is viewed as about to take place.

Aspect is indicated by the base form of the verb, $V$ plus an aspect marker. The marker of the perfect is *l;* of the imperfect, *t;* and of the prospective, *ṇar*.

Aspectual forms may be combined with the various forms of the auxiliary ( including the aspectual ) to produce a large variety of verb constructions. These are discussed in detail in the next chapter.

## 6. Verb derivation

Some verbs are derived from other verbs or from other parts of speech. For a discussion of verb derivation, see 11. D.

## B.   The Verb əs- ' to be '

### 1. Uses of əs-

The verb *əs-* ' to be ' is of special importance in Marathi.  As has already been mentioned, it is the only verb which has a full range of tenses: past, present, future, and habitual.  In addition, it can be used with the forms available to other verbs.  This chapter will present only the tense forms mentioned above.

Like its corresponding English  verb ' to be ' *əs-* has at least five distinct uses. Study the following examples. ( In these sentences *ahe* is the third person singular form of *əs-*. )

( a ) हा माझा भाऊ आहे.                   ha majha bhau ahe.
                                        This is my brother.

( b ) तो मुळ्गा हुशार आहे.               to mulga hušar ahe.
                                        That boy is bright.

( c ) माझी बहीण इथे आहे.                majhi bəhin ithe ahe.
                                        My sister is here.

( d ) देव आहे.                          dev ahe.
                                        God is ( God exists ).

( e ) मामा येणार आहे.                    mama yenar ahe.
                                        Uncle is coming.

In sentences ( a ) and ( b ) *əs-* is a copulative verb,  serving as a link between subject and predicate.  In sentence ( c ) it is used in  reference  to  location.  In sentence ( d ) it asserts existence. In sentence ( e ) it serves as an auxiliary of the main verb. When it is necessary to distinguish between the  various  uses  of *əs-* we shall use the following terms: copulative, locational, existential, and auxiliary. The term ' auxiliary ' when used without comment, however, will refer to *əs-* without reference to its distinct uses.

### 2. Present

The present tense of *əs-* is given in the paradigm below.*

*Paradigms throughout this book will not include *apən*. When *apən* is used for the second person it requires the same verb forms as *tumhi*. For the first person it requires the same forms as *amhi*.

| | |
|---|---|
| मी आहे | mi ahe |
| तू आहेस | tu ahes |
| तो आहे | to ahe |
| ती ” | ti ” |
| ते ” | te ” |
| आम्ही आहोत | amhi ahot |
| तुम्ही आहात | tumhi ahat |
| ते आहेत | te ahet |
| त्या आहेत | tya ” |
| ती ” | ṭi ” |

It can be seen that the gender of the subject does not affect the form of əs–. The above paradigm is summarized in Table 4.1.

Table 4.1.    *Present of əs–*

| Person | Singular | Plural |
|--------|----------|--------|
| 1 | ahe | ahot |
| 2 | ahes | ahat |
| 3 | ahe | ahet |

**Elided form.** In speech the *h* in *ahe* and *ahet* is generally elided, resulting in *ae* and *aet*. (This elision does not take place when əs– is used in its existential meaning or when special emphasis is placed on it.) In *ahot* and *ahat* the *h* is softened but does not entirely disappear.

**Negative.** The negative form of əs– is nəs–. The present tense of nəs– is given in the paradigm below.

| | | | |
|---|---|---|---|
| मी | नाही | mi | nahi |
| तू | नाहीस | tu | nahis |
| तो | नाही | to | nahi |
| ती | ” | ti | ” |
| ते | ” | te | ” |
| आम्ही | ” | amhi | ” |
| तुम्ही | ” | tumhi | ” |
| ते | नाहीत | te | nahit |
| त्या | ” | tya | ” |
| ती | ” | ti | ” |

These are summarized in Table 4.2.

Table 4.2.        *Present of nəs—*

| Person | Singular | Plural |
|--------|----------|--------|
| 1      | nahi     | nahi   |
| 2      | nahis    | ,,     |
| 3      | nahi     | nahit  |

**Alternate form of negative.** In the discussion above *nəs—* is treated as a negative verb. However, speakers frequently use *nahi* not as a negative verb but as an invariant adverb of negation, like Eng. 'not'. In this case *nahi* is used with the appropriate form of *əs—*, with əs— in its elided form.

| Underlying form | Spoken form |
|-----------------|-------------|
| mi nahi ahe | mi naie |
| tu nahi ahes | tu naies |
| to, ti, te nahi ahe | to, ti, te naie |
| amhi nahi ahot | amhi naiot |
| tumhi nahi ahat | tumhi naiat |
| te, tya, ti nahi ahat | te, tya, ti naiet |

## 3. Use of the present

**Contrast with imperfect A.** The present tense of *əs—* is used either to refer to a condition obtaining at the present moment, or to a general truth. It contrasts with the use of *əs—* in the imperfect A form ( see 5.C. 1.1 ). Though the imperfect A form has yet to be introduced it may be helpful to contrast the present and imperfect A forms of *əs—* here.[*]

ते ऑफिसात आहेत.

te ɔfisat aet.
He is in the office ( now ).

रोज दुपारी ते ऑफिसात असतात.

roj dupari te ɔfisat əstat.
Every afternoon he is in the office.

हे पुस्तक फार अवघड आहे.

he pustək phar əvghəḍ ae.
This book is very difficult.

[*]For further examples see Appendix C.

त्याची पुस्तकं नेहमीच अवघड असतात.  tyači pustəkə: nehmic əvghəd əstat.

His books are always difficult.

**Use of the present for the future**. As has already been mentioned, the time reference of tense forms is very flexible. The present forms of *əs*– and *nəs*– may be used to refer to a condition which is not true at the present moment but will be shortly, e. g.:

आज दुपारी मी इथे नाही आहे.  aj dupari mi ithe naie.

I will not be here this afternoon.

This flexibility is not peculiar to Marathi. In English also the above message might be conveyed with the present tense: ' I 'm not here this afternoon. '

## 4. Past

The stem* for the past affirmative of *əs*– is *hot*–; for the negative, *nəvht*–. The endings are the regular perfect endings for intransitive verbs ( see 5.C.2./1 ). The endings are presented below in Table 4.3.

Table 4.3.  *Past Endings of əs and nəs*–

| Person | Singular | | | Plural | | |
|--------|---|---|---|---|---|---|
| | M | F | N | M | F | N |
| 1 | o | e | – | o | o | – |
| 2 | as | is | – | a ( t ) | a ( t )***– | |
| 3 | a | i | ə: ** | e | ya | i |

Note that the third person endings are the regular adjective endings,

**Past affirmative**. The full forms of the past of *əs*– are given below.

| मी होतो | mi hoto (*m.*) |
| मी होते | mi hote (*f.*) |
| तू होतास | tu hotas (*m.*) |
| तू होतीस | tu hotis (*f.*) |

*A stem is a verb form to which an ending is added.

**As elsewhere, the neuter singular ending is *ə*: in the spoken form and *e* in the written.

***Parentheses are used in this book to indicate optional alternants. Thus, above the 2nd p. pl. ending may be either *a* or *at*.

| तो होता | to hota (*m.*) |
| ती होती | ti hoti (*f.*) |
| ते होतं | te hotə: (*n.*) |
| आम्ही होतो | amhi hoto |
| तुम्ही होता(त) | tumhi hota(t) |
| ते होते | te hote (*m.*) |
| त्या होत्या | tya hotya (*f.*) |
| ती होती | ti hoti (*n.*) |

**Past negative**. The full forms of the past of *nəs–* are given below.

| मी नव्हतो | mi nəvhto (*m.*) |
| मी नव्हते | mi nəvhte (*f.*) |
| तू नव्हतास | tu nəvhtas (*m.*) |
| तू नव्हतीस | tu nəvhtis (*f.*) |
| तो नव्हता | to nəvhtə (*m.*) |
| ती नव्हती | ti nəvhti (*f.*) |
| ते नव्हतं | te nəvhtə: (*n.*) |
| आम्ही नव्हतो | amhi nəvhto |
| तुम्ही नव्हता(त) | tumhi nəvhta(t) |
| ते नव्हते | te nəvhte (*m.*) |
| त्या नव्हत्या | tya nəvhtya (*f.*) |
| ती नव्हती | ti nəvhti (*n.*) |

**Use of the past**. The past of *əs–* and *nəs–* is used to refer to a particular moment in the past or to a general condition or a general truth. It is not, however, used in reference to a habitual state in the past. For the latter the habitual is used. See the next section for the contrast between the use of the past and the habitual.

## 5. Habitual

The stem for the habitual affirmative is *əs–*; for the negative *nəs–*. The habitual endings are presented in Table 4.4.

Table 4.4.  *Habitual Endings for ǝs– and nǝs–*

| Person | Singular | Plural |
|--------|----------|--------|
| 1 | e | u |
| 2 | ǝs | a |
| 3 | ǝ | ǝt |

**Habitual affirmative.** The full forms of the habitual of *ǝs–* are given below.

| | | | |
|---|---|---|---|
| मी असे | mi ǝse | | |
| तू असस | tu ǝsǝs | | |
| तो असे | to ǝse | | |
| ती ” | ti ” | | |
| ते ” | te ” | | |
| आम्ही असू | amhi ǝsu | | |
| तुम्ही असा | tumhi ǝsa | | |
| ते असत | te ǝsǝt | | |
| त्या ” | tya ” | | |
| ती ” | ti ” | | |

**Habitual negative.** The full forms of the habitual of *nǝs–* are given below.

| | |
|---|---|
| मी नसे | mi nǝse |
| तू नसस | tu nǝsǝs |
| तो नसे | to nǝse |
| ती ” | ti ” |
| ते ” | te ” |
| आम्ही नसू | amhi nǝsu |
| तुम्ही नसा | tumhi nǝsa |
| ते नसत | te nǝsǝt |
| त्या ” | tya ” |
| ती ” | ti ” |

**Contrast with past.** Note the difference in the use of the past and habitua forms of *ǝs–*.

आम्ही काल इथे होतो.　amhi kal ithe hoto.
We were here yesterday.

आम्ही लहानपणी तिथे असू.　amhi lǝhanpǝṇi tithe ǝsu.
We used to be there in childhood.

The habitual of the auxiliary is frequently found in writing. In speech, however, it is more likely to be replaced by the past habitual ( see 5.B.2 ).

## 6. Future

The stem for the future affirmative is *əs–*; for the negative, *nəs–*. The endings are the regular future endings ( see 5.B.1 ). The future endings for the auxiliary are presented in Table 4.5 below.

Table 4.5.   *Future Endings for əs– and nəs–*

| Person | Singular | Plural |
|--------|----------|--------|
| 1 | en | u |
| 2 | šil | al |
| 3 | el | til |

**Future ( affirmative ).** The full forms of the future of *əs–* are given below.

| मी असेन | mi əsen |
|---------|---------|
| तू असशील | tu əsšil |
| तो असेल | to əsel |
| ती ” | ti ” |
| ते ” | te ” |
| आम्ही असू | amhi əsu |
| तुम्ही असाल | tumhi əsal |
| ते असतील | te əstil |
| त्या ” | tya ” |
| ती ” | ti ” |

**Future ( negative ).** The full forms of the future of *nəs–* are given below.

| मी नसेन | mi nəsen |
|---------|----------|
| तू नसशील | tu nəsšil |
| तो नसेल | to nəsel |
| ती ” | ti ” |
| ते ” | te ” |
| आम्ही नसू | amhi nəsu |
| तुम्ही नसाल | tumhi nəsal |
| ते नसतील | te nəstil |
| त्या ” | tya ” |
| ती ” | ti ” |

**Use of the future.** The future tense of the auxiliary may be used simply to indicate futurity. Generally, however, an element of uncertainty is implied.

ते उद्या घरी असतील.  te udya ghəri əstil.

He will be home tomorrow.

He will probably be home tomorrow.

To express greater definiteness about the future, the prospective may be used ( see 5.C.3. ).

The future of the auxiliary may also be used to express uncertainty about the present.

ते आता घरी असतीळ.  te ata ghəri əstil.

He must be at home now.

## C.  Verb Forms

### 1. Basic verb forms

Most of the verbal constructions used in Marathi are combinations of one or more of the forms listed below, along with, in many cases, the auxiliary əs— which has already been introduced.

( a ) V–

( b ) V–i–

( c ) V–u

( d ) V–nə:

( e ) V–ayla

( f ) V–ayc–

( g ) V–un

( h ) V–av–

( i ) V–t

( j ) V–ṇar

( k ) V–l–

( a ) is the verbal base; ( b ) is the verbal base plus the stem formative *i*. ( c ) is used in a variety of constructions which cannot conveniently be given a label. ( d ) and ( e ) are verbal nouns and ( f ) is a verbal adjective. ( g ) serves as a subordinating conjunction; ( h ) is a modal* stem, used in constructions referring to obligation, desire, or uncertainty. ( i ), ( j ), and ( k ) are aspectual stems. ( i ) is used for the imperfect, ( j ) for the prospective, and ( k ) for the perfect.

It should be clear from the above description that taken by themselves these forms have little or no meaning. They acquire meaning only in the context of a given construction.

## 2. Application of morphophonemic rules

We have already seen in the discussion of noun forms that when stem formatives or endings are added to base forms, certain regular sound changes, called morphophonemic changes, occur. The rules for some of these changes are quite general; that is, they apply to all parts of speech. Whether they apply to a particular part of speech depends on the base endings found in that part of speech. For instance, a rule regarding bases ending in *e* will affect a number of Marathi verbs. A rule regarding monosyllabic bases ending in *u* will affect only one verb — *dhu* ' wash. ' A rule regarding bases of more than one syllable ending in *u* will not affect Marathi verbs at all.

The remainder of this section will merely list the basic verb forms and the constructions in which they are used, along with the relevant morphophonemic rules and the most common irregular bases. For a detailed discussion of each construction, consult the appropriate section. Refer to the index for page numbers. For a summary of morphophonemic rules see Appendix A.

## 3. Verb constructions

( 1 ) The verbal base as it stands is used as the familiar imperative.
*Irregular form*
*lih*–**. The familiar imperative is *lihi*.

In adding *a* to the base to form the respectful/plural imperative, some bases undergo changes.

---

\*Modal expressions are those that convey the speaker's attitude towards an action.

\*\*This verb actually has two base forms: *lihi*– when the base is used alone or before a consonant, *lih*– when it is used before a vowel. This alternation will be taken for granted in the remainder of the discussion.

Rule M₁

| | |
|---|---|
| घे– | ghe– |
| घ्या | ghya |
| पि– | pi– |
| प्या | pya |

The respectful/plural imperative of *ye–* is *ya.*

Rule M₃

| | |
|---|---|
| धु– | dhu– |
| धुवा | dhuva |

Rule M₄

| | |
|---|---|
| जा– | ja– |
| जा | ja |
| खा– | kha– |
| खा | kha |

( 2 ) V–i

    ( a )  Future

    ( b )  Habitual

    ( c )  V–i pəryəntə

A variant of *V–i* is *V–e.* The *i* stem is used with bases terminating in a vowel or a vowel plus *h*, and with most transitive verbs. For most other verbs the *e* stem is used.

*Examples of i stem*

| | |
|---|---|
| जा– | ja– ( ending in vowel ) |
| जाई– | jai– |
| राह्– | rah– ( ending in *h* ) |
| राही– | rahi– |
| कर– | kər– ( transitive ) |
| करी– | kəri– |

*Examples of e stem*

| | |
|---|---|
| पोच– | poc– ( intransitive ) |
| पोचे– | poce– |
| झोप– | jhop– ( intransitive ) |
| झोपे– | jhope– |

( 3 ) V–u

 ( a ) Imperative. The second person imperative forms have already been mentioned in (1) above. The imperative, however, has a complete paradigm for all persons and numbers.

 ( b ) V–u de–

 ( c ) V–u lag–

 ( d ) apən V–u ya

 ( e ) V–u nəye

 ( f ) V–u nəko(s), V–u nəka

 ( g ) V–u šək–

 ( h ) V–u pah–

   Rule $M_3$

    धु–       dhu–

    धुवू       dhuvu

( 4 ) V–nə:*

 ( a ) V–nə:

 ( b ) V–nya( nyaču̇ya ) + post.

 ( c ) V–nyat ye–

 ( d ) $V_1$–nyac–E** $V_2$

( 5 ) V–ayla

 ( a ) V–ayla

 ( b ) $V_1$–ayla $V_2$

 ( c ) V–ayla pahijə

 ( d ) V–ayla lag–

   Rule $M_1$

    घे–       ghe–

    घ्यायला     ghyayla

    पि–       pi–

    प्यायला     pyayla

   Rule $M_3$

    धु–       dhu–

    धुवायला     dhuvayla

*In written Marathi *V–ne* is used instead of *V–nə:*.

**E is used to indicate a variable ending.

Rule M₄

| जा– | ja– |
| जायला | jayla |
| खा– | kha– |
| खायला | khayla |

(6) V–ayc–

    (a) N  V–ayc–E

    (b) V–ayc–E  Aux

    (c) N–la (N–ni) V–ayc–E  Aux

    (d) V–ayc–E  N

    (e) V–ayčya + post.

    (f) V₁–ayc–E  V₂

Rule M₁

| घे– | ghe– |
| ध्यायचं | ghyaycə:* |
| पि– | pi– |
| प्यायचं | pyaycə: |

Rule M₃

| धु– | dhu– |
| धुवायचं | dhuvaycə: |

Rule M₄

| जा– | ja– |
| जायचं | jaycə: |
| खा– | kha– |
| खायचं | khaycə: |

(7) V–un

    (a) V₁–un V₂.   Subordinating conjunction, compound verb

    (b) N₁–kəḍun N₂ V–un ghe–

Rule M₃

| धु– | dhu– |
| धुवून | dhuvun |

---

\*Forms having variable endings are given as neuter singular in the examples.

( 8 ) V–av–

    ( a ) N  V–av–E

    ( b ) N–ni V–av–E

    ( c ) N–la V–av–E lag–

        Rule M₁

          घे–                  ghe–

          ध्यावं             ghyavə:

          पि–                  pi–

          प्यावं              pyavə:

        Rule M₃

          धु--                 dhu–

          धुवावं             dhuvavə:

        Rule M₄

          जा–                  ja–

          जावं               javə:

          खा–                  kha–

          खावं               khavə:

( 9 ) V–t

    ( a ) V–t–E$_{imf}$

    ( b ) V–t  Aux

    ( c ) V–ta V–ta

    ( d ) V–t

    ( e ) V–tac

    ( f ) nə: V–ta

    ( g ) V–tana

    ( h ) V–ta ye–

    ( i ) V–ta kama nəye

    ( j ) V–t–E ahe

    ( k ) cal–t–E ho

    ( l ) V–t–E N

    ( m ) V–t ja

    ( n ) V–t əslel–E N

The following rule applies only to the imperfect B where *V–t* is used without any termination: verbal bases ending in a consonant require the addition of *ə* or *i* before the addition of *t*. For most verbs the vowel used is *ə*.

|  |  |
|---|---|
| ऐक्र– | əik– |
| ऐकत | əikət |
| पळ– | pəḷ– |
| पळत | pəḷət |

A common verb that usually uses *i* instead of *ə* is *kər–*.

|  |  |
|---|---|
| कर– | kər– |
| करीत | kərit |

(10) V–ṇar

    ( a ) V–ṇar Aux

    ( b ) V–ṇar–E  N

(11) V–l–

    ( a ) V–l–E  Aux

    ( b ) V–l–E  əst–E

    ( c ) V–l–E  pahijə

    ( d ) V–lel–E

    ( e ) V–lel–E  bər–E

    ( f ) V–lel–E  N

    ( g ) $V_1$–lel–E  $V_2$

    ( h ) V–l–E  nə:  V–l–E

    ( i ) V–lya  V–lya

    ( j ) V–lya + post.

    ( k ) $V_1$–lyac–E  $V_2$

A number of bases have irregular stems before *l*.

|  |  |
|---|---|
| जा– | ja– |
| गे– | ge– |
| ये– | ye– |
| आ– | a– |
| कर– | kər– |
| के– | ke– |
| मर– | mər– |
| मे– | me– |

| देـ     | de-      |
| दिـ     | di-      |
| घेـ     | ghe-     |
| घेतـ    | ghet-    |
| घालـ    | ghal-    |
| घातـ    | ghat-    |
| बघ     | bəgh     |
| बघितـ  | bəghit-  |
| मागـ    | mag-     |
| मागित   | magit-   |
| सांगـ    | saŋg-    |
| सांगितـ  | saŋgit-  |
| धुـ     | dhu-     |
| धुतـ    | dhut-    |
| म्हणـ    | mhəṇ-*   |
| म्हटـ    | mhəṭ-    |
| खाـ     | kha-     |
| खालـ    | khal-    |
| पाहـ    | pah-     |
| पाहिـ    | pahi-    |
| राहـ    | rah-     |
| राहिـ    | rahi-    |
| वाहـ    | vah-     |
| वाहिـ    | vahi-    |
| मिळـ    | miḷ-     |
| मिळाـ    | miḷa-    |
| पळـ     | pəḷ-     |
| पळाـ    | pəḷa-    |

---

*The irregular *mhəṭ* is used when *mhəṇ-* is treated as a transitive verb in the perfect: *tyani mhəṭlə:*. The regular *mhəṇala* is used when the verb is treated as an intransitive.

| निघ– | nigh– |
| निघा– | nigha– |
| ऊड– | uḍ– |
| उडा– | uḍa– |
| पि– | pi– |
| प्याय– | pyay–* |
| गा– | ga– |
| गाय– | gay– |
| ले– | le– |
| ल्याय | lyay– |
| वि– | vi– |
| व्याय– | vyay– |
| हो– | ho– |
| झा– | jha– |

---

*The regular stem *pi*– is used by some speakers. In this case the ending is governed by the normal rules for transitive verbs. If *pyay*– is used, however, the word is treated as a special transitive verb.

# Chapter five

# SIMPLE SENTENCES

A.  Basic Patterns

1.  $N_1$  $N_2$  *(Aux)*.                $N_1$ is $N_2$. *

ती पाभर आहे.                    ti pabhər ae.
                                   That is a seed drill.

तो दवाखाना आहे.               to dəvakhana ae.
                                   That is a hospital.

तो माणूस आहे.                to maṇus ae.
                                   He is a man.

Often the auxiliary is omitted.

हा माझा भाऊ.                ha majha bhau.
                                   This is my brother.

2.  $N_1$  *mhəṇje*  $N_2$.              $N_1$ means $N_2$.
        *bərober*                         equals

This pattern is slightly different from 1 above. In 1, the relationship between $N_1$ and $N_2$ is that of identification; that is, we are asserting that $N_1$ belongs to a certain set of things. In 2, the relationship is one of equation; that is, two different items are asserted to have the same value.

* The formula on the right is for the corresponding English sentence.

| | |
|---|---|
| *brother* म्हणजे भाऊ. | *brother* mhənje *bhau.*<br>*Brother* means *bhau.* |
| दोन अधिक दोन बरोबर चार. | don ədhik don bərobər čar.<br>Two plus two equals four. |

3. *N A Aux.*  —  N is A.

| | |
|---|---|
| घर मोठं आहे. | ghər mothə: ae.<br>The house is big. |
| पुस्तक चांगलं आहे. | pustək cəŋglə: ae.<br>The book is good. |
| तो उंच आहे. | to uncə ae.<br>He is tall. |

4. *N Adv. Aux.* — N is Adv.
   *N₁ N₂–post. Aux.* — N₁ is prep. N₂.

| | |
|---|---|
| ऑफिस सिनेमासमोर आहे. | ɔfis sinemasəmor ae.<br>The office is in front of the theater. |

The adverb or postpositional phrase may precede the subject.

| | |
|---|---|
| त्याच्याजवळ पैसे आहेत. | tyačyajəvəl paise aet.<br>He has money.<br>( Lit., ' money is near him. ' ) |
| तिला मुलगा आहे. | tila mulga ae.<br>She has a son. |

5. *mi V–u ka?* — Shall ( should ) I V ?
   *amhi V–u ka?* — Shall ( should ) we V ?

| | |
|---|---|
| मी ते घेऊ का? | mi te gheu ka ?<br>Shall I take it ? |
| मी सुरू करू का? | mi suru kəru ka ?<br>Shall I begin ? |
| आम्ही तिकडे जाऊ का? | amhi tikde jau ka ?<br>Should we go there ? |

Strictly speaking, this and the following pattern contain the first person of the imperative paradigm ( see section B.6 of this chapter ). However, as the first person imperative and second person imperative discussed in section 7 below require special sentence patterns, they are treated separately from the remainder of the paradigm.

6.  *mi K V–u?*                     Question word shall I V ?
    *amhi* "                       Question word shall we V ?

    मी कुठे जाऊ ?                    mi kuṭhe jau ?
                                    Where shall I go ?

    मी किती वाजता येऊ ?              mi kiti vajta yeu ?
                                    What time shall I come ?

    आम्ही ते केव्हा पाठवू ?          amhi te kevhā paṭhvu ?
                                    When should we send it ?

7.  (1) *V.*                        V.

This is the second person imperative. The simple verb base *V* serves as the familiar, *V–a* as the respectful/plural.

    चल.             cəl.            Come on.*
    चला.            cəla.           "

This pattern may be expanded with a direct object.

    (2) *N V.*                      V N.

    चहा घे.         čəha ghe.       Take some tea.
    चहा घ्या.       čəha ghya.      "

It may also be expanded with adverbs of place, time, or manner.

    (3) *Adv. V.*                   V Adv.

    तिकडे जा.       tikḍe ja.       Go there.
    तिकडे जा.       tikḍe ja.       "
    आठ वाजता ये.    aṭh vajta ye.   Come at eight o' clock.
    आठ वाजता या.    aṭh vajta ya.   "
    हळू बोल.        həḷu bol.       Speak softly.
    हळू बोला.       həḷu bola.      "

*The first sentence in each set is in the familiar, the second in the respectful/plural.

Patterns ( 2 ) and ( 3 ) may be combined.*

| | | |
|---|---|---|
| पुस्तक उद्या ने. | pustək udya ne. | Take the book tomorrow. |

The negative form of the familiar imperative is *V–u nəko(s)*. For the respectful/plural the form is *V–u nəka*.

| | | |
|---|---|---|
| ते करू नको ( नको ). | te kəru nəkos (nəko). | Don't do that. |
| ते करू नका. | te kəru nəka. | ” |

8.  *apəṇ V–u ya*\*\*      Let's V.

आपण त्यांच्याकडे जाऊ या.     apəṇ tyančyakəde jau ya.
Let's go to his place.

आपण उद्या सुरू करू या.     apəṇ udya suru kəru ya.
Let's start tomorrow.

आपण हुतुतू खेळू या.     apəṇ hututu kheḷu ya.
Let's play hututu.

This construction has no corresponding negative. A negative reply to the first sentence above might take one of the following forms.

नको, आपण इथे थांबू या.     nəko, apəṇ ithe thambu ya.
No, let's stay here.

त्यांच्याकडे जायला नको.     tyančyakəde jayla nəko.
Let's not go to his place.

9.  *V–ayc–E*

This is an impersonal construction with no exact English equivalent. It is particularly used in giving directions or in describing how something is to be done. Study the following example.

सरळ जायचं त्या देवीच्या देवळापर्यंत.     sərəḷ jaycə:, tya devičya devḷa-
तिथे डावीकडे वळून एक फर्लांग जायचं.     pəryəntə. tithe ḍavikəde vəlun
     ek phərlaŋ jaycə·.

*For order in sentences involving several adverbs, see Appendix D.

\*\*In any sentence pattern a verb may be modified by adverbs. Moreover, a transitive verb will necessarily have an object. From here on, these possible expansions will be taken for granted and will not be specifically indicated in the formulas for sentence patterns.

Go straight up to the temple of
the goddess.  Then turn left and
go one furlong.

If there is a direct object, the ending of V–ayc-E must agree with the object
in gender and number.   The endings are the regular adjective endings. Note the
agreement in the following description of how to prepare *methi*, a leafy vegetable.

मेथी आणि कांदे चिरायचे. फोडणी
करून त्यात भाजी शिजवून घ्यायची.
मग मीठ आणि बेसन घालून आणखी
थोडा वेळ शिजवून चुलीवरून उतरून
घ्यायची.

methi aṇi kande čirayce.[*] phodṇi
kərun tyat bhaji šijvun ghyayči.
məg miṭh aṇi besən ghalun aṇkhi
thoḍa veḷ šijvun culivərun utrun
ghyayči.

Cut up the vegetable and onions.
Put oil and spices in the pan and
cook the vegetable in them. Then
add salt and gram flour and cook
a little longer. Then remove from
the stove.

## 10.  *N  V.*                             N V.

The greatest number of Marathi sentences are of this pattern, in  which  *N*  is
the subject and *V* the predicate. Within this  general pattern there are two forms
of verb construction: unitary and participial. In a unitary construction  all  information about the action is  contained  in a  single verb form.  In a participial
construction a participle is used along with the auxiliary.  The participle indicates
the aspect  and the auxiliary  generally  indicates tense. However, the auxiliary
may also be used in an aspectual form to convey a particular nuance of an action.

The section below is arranged according to the forms of construction within the
general *N V* pattern. Since there are differences in sentence pattern depending on
whether a verb is transitive, intransitive, or *N–la* impersonal, examples of sentences
with each verb type will be given. Whenever *əs–* can be used  as a main  verb in
a particular construction, an example will also be given.

---

[*] Note that when there are two direct objects the verb is governed by the
nearer one.

## B. Unitary Constructions

### 1. The future

The future is used for actions felt as somewhat remote.[*] The actual time of the action may be imminent, but it is not felt as immediate or definite. The formula for this construction is:

$$N \quad V\text{--}E_f$$

where $E_f$ stands for the set of future endings presented in Table 5.1 below.

Table 5.1.    *Future Endings*

| Person | Singular | | Plural |
|--------|----------|-----|--------|
| 1 | in | en | u |
| 2 | šil | | al |
| 3 | il, | el | til |

The endings *in* and *il* are used after a base ending in a vowel, or a vowel plus *h*, and with most transitive verbs. For other verbs *en* and *el* are used.

The full paradigm for *ja–* ' to go ' is given below.

| | |
|---|---|
| मी जाईन | mi jain |
| तू जाशील | tu jašil |
| तो जाईल | to jail |
| ती ” | ti ” |
| ते ” | te ” |
| आम्ही जाऊ | amhi jau |
| तुम्ही जाल | tumhi jal |
| ते जातील | te jatil |
| त्या ” | tya ” |
| ती ” | ti ” |

*Intransitive*

तो पुढच्या वर्षी अमेरिकेश जाईल.    to puḍhčya vərši əmerikela jail.

He will go to America next year.

---

[*] The construction described here is the unitary future construction. For the immediate future the prospective is used ( see 5.C.3. ).

*Transitive*

मी उद्या हे काम संपवीन.                          mi udya he kam səmpvin.

                                                 I will finish this work tomorrow.

### N–la Impersonal

The formula for the future with N–la impersonal verbs is:

$$N_1-la \quad N_2 \quad V-E_f$$

The ending is governed by $N_2$ and will be in the third person singular or plural.

आम्हाला माल उद्या मिळेल.                         amhala mal udya miḷel.

                                                 We will receive the goods tomorrow.

आम्हाला फुलं उद्या मिळतील.                        amhala phulə: udya miḷtil.

                                                 We will receive the flowers tomorrow.

### Auxiliary

The future of the auxiliary has already been given ( see 4.B.6 ).

**Negative.** The future has no corresponding negative. The negative is that of the prospective ( see 5.C.3 ).

मी जाणार नाही.                                   mi jaṇar nahi.

                                                 I will not go.

मी ते करणार नाही.                                 mi te kərṇar nahi.

                                                 I will not do it.

आम्हाला पुस्तकं वेळेवर मिळणार                        amhala pustəkə: veḷevər miḷṇar
नाहीत.                                           nahit.

                                                 We will not receive the books on time.

## 2. The past habitual

As its name implies, the past habitual is used for habitual action in the past, much as ' used to ' is in English. The formula for this construction is:

$$N \quad V-ayc-E_{ph}$$

where $E_{ph}$ indicates the set of past habitual endings presented in Table 5.2. These agree with the subject $N$.

Table 5.2. *Past Habitual Endings*

| Person | Singular | | | Plural | | |
|:---:|:---:|:---:|:---:|:---:|:---:|:---:|
| | M | F | N | M | F | N |
| 1 | o | e | | o | o | |
| 2 | as | is | | a | a | |
| 3 | a | i | ə: | e | ya | i |

These endings are the same as those for the perfect of intransitive verbs ( see section C.2./1 of this chapter ). Note that the third person endings are the regular adjective endings.

Some speakers tend to use the past habitual only in the third person. Other speakers use it more freely. ( The alternative form for expressing the same meaning is *V–t əse*. For this form see section C.1./2 of this chapter ).

The full paradigm of *ja-* ' to go ' is given below.

| | |
|---|---|
| मी जायचो | mi jayco *(m.)* |
| मी जायचे | mi jayce *(f.)* |
| तू जायचास | tu jaycas *(m.)* |
| तू जायचीस | tu jayčis *(f.)* |
| तो जायचा | to jayca |
| ते जायचं | te jaycə: *(n.)* |
| ती जायची | ti jayči* *(f.)* |
| आम्ही जायचो | amhi jayco *(m., f.)* |
| तुम्ही जायचा | tumhi jayca *(m, f.)* |
| ते जायचे | te jayce *(m.)* |
| त्या जायच्या | tya jayčya |
| ती जायची | ti jayči *(n.)* |

*Intransitive*

ती पूर्वी तिकडे जायची.   ti purvi tikḍe jayči.

   She used to go there.

* The change of *c* to *č* is due to the operation of Rule $M_5$: *c, j,* and *s* become respectively *č, ǰ,* and *š* before the addition of *i* or *y,* and optionally before the addition of *e.*

*Transitive*

पूर्वी तो शेतात काम करायचा.            purvi to šetat kam kərayca.

                                      Formerly he used to work in the field.

*N–la Impersonal*

लहानपणी त्याची पुस्तकं मला            ləhanpaṇi tyaci pustəkə: məla avḍayči.

आवडायची.                             In childhood I used to like his books.

*Auxiliary*

इथे पूर्वी झाडी असायची.               ithe purvi jhaḍi əsayči.

                                      There used to be  trees here.


## 3. The desiderative

The desiderative is used to express mild  obligation.  It corresponds roughly to some uses of English *should*.  The construction  may be either personal or impersonal.

**Personal.**  The formula for the personal is:

$$N_1\text{--}ni \ (N_2) \ V\text{--}av\text{--}E_d$$

where $E_d$ indicates the set of desiderative  verb endings.  The  choice of ending is governed by $N_2$, the direct object.  If there is no direct object the ending is neuter singular.  Note that the  subject is in the instrumental;  that is,  it is followed by the instrumental postposition *ni*.

Since agreement is with the  direct object the desiderative endings are limited to the third person.  They are given in Table 5.3 below.


Table 5.3.  *Desiderative Endings*

|        | Singular |        |        | Plural |        |
|--------|----------|--------|--------|--------|--------|
| M      | F        | N      | M      | F      | N      |
| a      | i        | ə:     | e(t)   | ya(t)  | i(t)   |


Note that these are the regular adjective endings  except that the plural  forms may have *t* added.

If the subject is in the second person, an ending  agreeing  with  the subject is sometimes added to that agreeing with the object.   The second person singular ending is *s*; the second person plural ending is *t*. The singular ending is regularly used, the plural ending only rarely.

### Intransitive

मुलांनी आईवडिलांकडे रहावं.

mulanni aivədlaŋkəde rəhavə:.
Children should stay with their parents.

तू इथे रहावंस.

tu ithe rəhavə:s.
You should stay here.

### Transitive

सरकारनी लोकांना मदत करावी.

sərkarni lokanna mədət kəravi.
The government should help the people.

### N–la Impersonal

पाहुण्यांना हा पदार्थ आवडावा.

pahuṇyanna ha pədarthə avḍava.
The guest should like this dish.

### Auxiliary

तुम्ही आनंदात असावं.

tumhi anəndat əsavə:.
You should be happy.

**Negative.** The negative of this construction is:

$$N_1\text{-}ni \quad (N_2) \quad V\text{-}u \quad nəye$$

If the direct object is plural a *t* is added to *nəye*. If the subject ( $N_1$ ) is in the second person, *nəye* generally agrees with the subject rather than the object. In this case the ending is *s* in the singular and *t* in the plural.

वीस वर्षांच्या आत मुलांनी लग्न करू नये.

vis vəršančya at mulinni ləgnə kəru nəye.
Girls should not marry before twenty.

तू पैसे घालवू नयेस.

tu pəise ghalvu nəyes.
You should not waste money.

**Impersonal.** The impersonal construction is used for general statements about things to be done. The corresponding English sentences are usually expressed in the passive or with the impersonal ' one, ' ' people, ' etc.

The formula for the impersonal desiderative is:

$$(N_2)\quad V\text{-}av\text{-}E_d$$

The ending is governed by $N_2$, the direct object. If there is no direct object the ending is neuter singular.

*Intransitive*

सकाळी लवकर उठावं.                             səkaḷi ləvkər uṭhavə:.
                                              One should get up early in the morning.

*Transitive*

पिकांना पुरेसं खत टाकावं.                       pikanna puresə: khət ṭakavə:.
                                              Sufficient fertilizer should be applied to crops.

*N–la Impersonal*

सर्बांना पुरेसे पैसे मिळावेत.                    sərvanna purese pəise miḷavet.
                                              Everyone should get enough money.

*Auxiliary*

नेहमी कामात असावं.                            nehemi kamat əsavə:.
                                              One should always be busy.

**Negative.** The negative of this construction is:

$$(N_2)\quad V\text{-}u\ nəye$$

दुपारच्या उन्हात हिंडू नये.                      duparčya unhat hiṇḍu nəye.
                                              One should not go about in the afternoon sun.

## 4. The subjunctive

The subjunctive is not much used in modern Marathi, but it is still required in certain instances. It is, however, restricted to the third person, and is mainly used to indicate indefiniteness or uncertainty. It is also used in figurative speech. Corresponding sentences in English often have expressions like ' as if, ' ' most likely, ' or ' might. ' The subjunctive is also used for repeated actions. The corresponding English sentences for these usually have ' would V. '

The form of the subjunctive construction depends on whether the verb is intransitive or transitive.

**Intransitive verbs and auxiliary.** For intransitive verbs and the auxiliary the form of the subjunctive is

$$N \quad V\text{-}av\text{-}E_{subjunct}$$

where $E_{subjunct}$ indicates the set of subjunctive endings presented in Table 5.4. The endings are governed by the subject $N$. If there is no subject ( that is, if the sentence is impersonal ), the verb is neuter singular.

Table 5.4. *Subjunctive Endings*

|  | Singular |  |  | Plural |  |
|---|---|---|---|---|---|
| M | F | N | M | F | N |
| a | i | ə: | e(t) | ya(t) | i(t) |

Note that these endings are the same as the desiderative endings.

*Intransitive*

थोड्या वेळानी तो यावा.   thoḍya veḷani to yava.
He should be here in a short time.

*Auxiliary*

तो राम असावा.   to ram əsava.
That must be Ram.

**Negative.** For the negative of the auxiliary, the negative verb *nəs-* is used.

ह्या परीक्षेत पास होणं फारसं   hya pərikšet pas honə: pharsə:
अवघड नसावं.   əvghəḍ nəsavə:.

It's probably not very difficult to pass in this exam.

The negative subjunctive of intransitive verbs is not generally encountered.

**Transitive verbs.** For transitive verbs the subjunctive is identical to the desiderative.

त्यांनी घोड्यावर बसायचा प्रयत्न   tyanni ghoḍyavər bəsayca prəyətnə
करावा आणि घोडा पळावा असं   kərava aṇi ghoḍa pəḷava əsə:
बराच वेळ चाललं होतं.   bərac veḷ callə: hotə:.

He would try to sit on the horse
and the horse would run away.
This went on for quite a while.

**Negative.**  The negative of this form, like that of the desiderative, is *V–u nəye*. The same rules of agreement apply.


## 5. The habitual

The habitual of verbs other than the auxiliary is not commonly used in speech, but it is used in written narration. Even then it is generally restricted to the first and third person singular and the third person plural.

The habitual is used for habitual action in the past. It corresponds roughly to English ' would V. '

The formula for the habitual is:

$$N \quad V–E_{hab}$$

where $E_{hab}$ stands for the set of habitual endings.

The stem of the habitual is *V*.  The endings are presented in Table 5.5 below.

Table 5.5.   *Habitual Endings*

| Person | Singular | Plural |
|--------|----------|--------|
| 1 | i, e* | - |
| 2 | – | - |
| 3 | i, e | t, ət, it ** |

The first person singular and third person forms of *ja–* ' to go ' are given below.

| | |
|---|---|
| मी जाई | mi jai |
| तो जाई | to jai |
| ती  ” | ti jai |
| ते  ” | te jai (*n.*) |
| ते जात | te jat (*m.*) |
| त्या  ” | tya  ” |
| ती  ” | ti  ”  (*n.*) |

*For the conditions governing this variation, see 4.C.3./2.

**Verbal bases ending in a vowel require *t*; those ending in a consonant generally require *ət*. One exception is *kər–*, for which the ending is *it*.

Rather than isolated sentences, a paragraph of narration will give a better idea of the use of the habitual. The following paragraph is taken from Vyankatesh Madgulkar's *maṇdesi̭ maṇsǝ:*.*

देशगांडे मास्तर फारच गंभीर होते. क्वचित ते विनोद करित. पण तो देखील गंभीर असे. ते आरोग्यशास्त्र शिकवू लागले की माझे डोळे जड होऊन मिटू लागत. पण पुस्तक पुढे धरून मी बसल्या बसल्या बैलासारखा झोप येई. कधी कधी ते मास्तरांच्या ध्यानात येई. पुस्तक खाली ठेऊन ते दोन्ही हातांचे तळवे एकमेकांवर चोळत आणि गंभीरपणे म्हणत, " तेलीबुवा, उठा, डोळ्याला पाणी लावून या आणि मग बसा. "

despaṇde mastǝr pharǝc gǝmbhir hote. kvǝcit te vinod *kǝrit*, pǝṇ to dekhil gǝmbhir *ǝse*. te arogyǝśastrǝ śikvu lagle ki majhe ḍoḷe jǝḍ houn miṭu *lagǝt*. pǝṇ pustǝk puḍhe dhǝrun mi bǝslya bǝslya bailasarkha jhop *ghei*. kǝdhi kǝdhi te mastǝrancya dhyanat *yei*. pustǝk khali ṭheun te donhi hatance tǝḷve ekmekaṽvǝr *colǝt* aṇi gǝmphirpǝṇe *mhǝnǝt*, " telibuva, uṭha. ḍoḷyala paṇi laun ya aṇi mǝg bǝsa. "

Deshpande Master was very serious. He rarely made a joke, but if he did, even that was serious. When he started to teach physiology my eyes would get heavy and start to close. But I would hold my book in front of me and sleep sitting straight up, like a bullock. Master would realize this. Then he would put his book down, rub his hands together, and say gravely," Teli, get up. Go splash some water in your eyes and then sit down. "

**Negative**. The negative habitual of the auxiliary is *nǝse*. For other words the negative meaning of the habitual is conveyed not with this form but with the construction *V–t nǝse*.

There is in form a negative counterpart for the habitual, but it has a slightly different meaning from what would be expected. This form is limited to the third person. In the singular it is *V–ina* ( or *V–ena* )**, in the plural *V–inat* ( or *V–enat* ). This form is used for repeated action.

| | |
|---|---|
| मी पुन्हा पुन्हा दार उघडायचा प्रयत्न केला पण ते उघडेना. | mi punha punha dar ughḍayca prǝyǝtnǝ kela pǝṇ te ughḍena. |
| | I tried again and again to open the door but it wouldn't open. |

---

*Vyankatesh Madgulkar, *maṇdeśi maṇsǝ:*. (Poona: Continental Prakashan, 1941.) The chapter from which the above selection is taken is included in our *Intermediate Marathi Reader*.

** See the rules for variation of *V–i* and *V–e* presented in 4.C.3./2.

मी पुष्कळदा त्याला सांगितलं पण          mi puškəɭda tyala saŋgitlə: pəṇ to
तो अभ्यास करीना.                          əbhyas kərina.

                                         I told him to many times but he
                                         wouldn't study.

## 6. The imperative

The first and second person forms of the imperative have already been
introduced. The remaining forms are much less frequently used. They occur
primarily in prayers, blessings, etc. The corresponding English sentences often
have the form ' May N  V ' or ' Let N  V. '

The formula for the third person imperative is:

$$N \quad V-E_{imp}$$

where $E_{imp}$ indicates the set of third person imperative endings. The ending of
the verb is governed by the subject. The endings are presented in Table
5.6 below.

Table 5.6.  *Third Person Imperative Endings*

| Singular | Plural |
|----------|--------|
| o        | ot     |

The third person imperative forms of *kər–* ' to do ' are given below.

| करो  | kəro  |
|------|-------|
| करोत | kərot |

*Intransitive*

तुझ्या तोंडात साखर पडो !                   tujhya toṇḍat sakhər pəḍo !*
                                         May sugar fall into your mouth !

*Transitive*

देव तुझं भलं करो !                        dev tujhə: bhələ: kəro !
                                         May God bless you !

*N-la Impersonal*

तुला बरं वाटो !                           tula bərə: vaṭo !
                                         May you feel well !

―――――――――
*This is said when someone predicts something good.

*Auxiliary*

असो. . əso.

So be it.

हवं असो वा नसो. həvə: əso va nəso.

Whether ( one ) wants it or not.

## C.   Participial Constructions

As we have already observed, some of the unitary verb constructions already introduced belong to the archaic structure of the language and have almost passed out of use. The participial constructions, on the other hand, belong to the living structure of the language. The forms can be put together in a large number of permutations and combinations. The number is so large that it would be difficult to list them all, and it would be unnecessary, for the meaning of the constructions is usually evident from the meaning of their constituent parts. Moreover, not all forms are of equal acceptability. Some are definitely acceptable, some are definitely unacceptable, but there is a residue about which even educated speakers could probably not agree. This is the situation not only in Marathi but in every language, and is, in fact, one of the factors that makes change and development in language possible.

### 1. The imperfect

As we have seen, action in the imperfect is viewed as incomplete. This action may be viewed as either habitual or incomplete. For these two different views of the imperfect there are two different forms, which have been termed in this book imperfect A and B.

( 1 ) **Imperfect A.** Imperfect A is used for habitual action. It has no auxiliary. Its formula is:

$$N \quad V{-}t{-}E_{imf}$$

where $E_{imf}$ indicates the set of endings for imperfect A presented in Table 5.7. The ending is governed by the subject, $N$.

Table 5.7.   *Imperfect A Endings*

| Person | Singular | | | Plural |
|--------|---|---|---|--------|
|        | M | F | N |        |
| 1      | o | e |   | o |
| 2      | os | es |   | a |
| 3      | o | e | ə: | at |

The full paradigm of *ja–* ' to go, ' is given below.

| | |
|---|---|
| मी जातो | mi jato (*m.*) |
| मी जाते | mi jate (*f.*) |
| तू जातोस | tu jatos (*m.*) |
| तू जातेस | tu jates (*f.*) |
| तो जातो | to jato |
| ती जाते | ti jate |
| ते जातं | te jatə: |
| आम्ही जातो | amhi jato |
| तुम्ही जाता | tumhi jata |
| ते जातात | te jatat |
| त्या जातात | tya jatat |
| ती जातात | ti jatat |

*Intransitive*

तो रोज आमच्याकडे येतो.            to roj amčyakəde yeto.
                                 He comes to our place daily.

ते वर्षातनं दोनदा पंढरपूरला       te vəršatnə: donda pəndhərpurla jatat.
जातात.                           They go to Pandharpur twice a year.

*Transitive*

तो कारखान्यात नोकरी करतो.         to karkhanyat nokri kərto.
                                 He works in the factory.

तो मराठी शिकवतो.                 to mərathi šikəvto.
                                 He teaches Marathi.

*N–la Impersonal*

तिला मराठी समजतं.                tila mərathi səməjtə:.
                                 She understands Marathi.

त्याला सिनेमा आवडतो.

tyala sinema avədto.

He enjoys movies.

*Auxiliary*

माझी बहीण मुंबईला असते.

majhi bəhiṇ mumbəila əste.

My sister lives in Bombay.

अमेरिकेमधे पुष्कळ इमारती दगडी असतात.

əmerikemədhe puškəl imarəti dəgḍi əstat.

Many buildings in America are of stone.

The imperfect A is limited to the affirmative and to the present tense. For the negative and for other tenses it must borrow from the regular imperfect B.

( 2 ) **Imperfect B**. This form of the imperfect is used primarily for action viewed as in progress. Its formula is:

$$N \quad V\text{-}t \quad Aux$$

The auxiliary may be used in the past, present, future, habitual, imperfect A, prospective, subjunctive, and other forms. Examples given here will be limited to the forms just mentioned.

*Intransitive*

तो तिकडे जात आहे.

to tikḍe jat ae.

He is going there. ( Right now he's on the way. )

तो तिकडे जात होता.

to tikḍe jat hota.

He was going there. ( He was on the way. ) He used to go there.

तो तिकडे जात असेल.

to tikḍe jat əsel.

He probably goes there. He is probably going there. ( He's probably on the way right now. )

तो तिकडे जात असे.

to tikḍe jat əse.

He used to go there.

तो तिकडे जात असतो.*

to tikḍe jat əsto.
He keeps going there.

तो तिकडे जात असणार.

to tikḍe jat əsṇar.
He probably goes there.
He is probably going there.

तो तिकडे जात असावा.

to tikḍe jat əsava.
He probably goes there.
He is probably going there.

*Transitive*

तो शेतात काम करीत आहे.

to šetat kam kərit ae.
He is working in the field.

तो शेतात काम करीत होता.

to šetat kam kərit hota.
He was working in the field.
He used to work in the field.

तो शेतात काम करीत असेल.

to šetat kam kərit əsel.
He's probably working in the field.
He probably works in the field.
He will probably be working in the
field.

तो शेतात काम करीत असे.

to šetat kam kərit əse.
He used to work in the field.

तो शेतात काम करीत असतो.

to šetat kam kərit əsto.
He regularly works in the field.

तो शेतात काम करीत असणार.

to šetat kam kərit əsṇar.
He is probably working in the field.
He probably works in the field.
He will probably be working in the
field.

---

* Some speakers might object to this sentence. It sounds more natural as a
question: *to tikḍe ka jat əsto ?* ' Why does he keep going there ? '

| तो शेतात काम करीत असावा. | to šetat kam kərit əsava. |
| | He is probably working in the field.* |
| | He probably works in the field. |

### N–la Impersonal

Generally, impersonal verbs are not used in this construction. This is similar to the rule in English prohibiting the formation of such sentences as ' I am wanting, ' ' I am understanding, ' etc.

### Auxiliary

The auxiliary also cannot be used in the imperfect B, as its meaning is ' to be ' and not ' to become. ' For the meaning ' to become ' the verb *ho–* is used.

| हल्ली दिवस लांब होत आहे. | həlli divəs lamb hot ae. |
| | Recently the day is getting long. |

**Negative.** The negative of imperfect B is formed according to the formula:

$$N \quad V{-}t \quad Aux_{neg}$$

This form also serves as the negative of imperfect A. Possibly to preserve the contrast between the imperfect A and B, there is a special form for the first person negative imperfect B :

$$N \quad V{-}t \quad nahi \ Aux$$

### Intransitive

| तो तिकडे जात नाही आहे. | to tikḍe jat nahie. |
| | He isn't going there. |
| तो तिकडे जात नाही. | to tikḍe jat nahi. |
| | He doesn't go there. |
| तो तिकडे जात नव्हता. | to tikḍe jat nəvhta. |
| | He wasn't going there ( at that time ). |
| तो तिकडे जात नसेल. | to tikḍe jat nəsel. |
| | He's probably not going there. |
| | He probably doesn't go there. |
| तो तिकडे जात नसे. | to tikḍe jat nəse. |
| | He did not use to go there. |

---

*This set has three sentences translated ' He is probably working in the field. ' The sentence with *əsel* is neutral. The use of *əsṇar* implies more certainty, the use of *əsava* less.

*Transitive*

तो शेतात काम करीत नाही आहे.  to šetat kam kərit nahie.

He isn't working in the field.

तो शेतात काम करीत नाही.  to šetat kam kərit nahi.

He doesn't work in the field.

तो शेतात काम करीत नव्हता.  to šetat kam kərit nəvhta.

He wasn't working in the field.

तो शेतात काम करीत नसेल.  to šetat kam kərit nəsel.

He's probably not working in the field. He probably doesn't work in the field. He probably will not be working in the field.

तो शेतात काम करीत नसे.  to šetat kam kərit nəse.

He didn't use to work in the field.

### N–la Impersonal

Since *N–la* impersonal verbs are rarely used in the imperfect B construction, the negative formula serves only for imperfect A.

तिला मराठी समजत नाही.  tila mərathi səmjət nahi.

She doesn't understand Marathi.

त्याला सिनेमा आवडत नाही.  tyala sinema avḍət nahi.

He doesn't enjoy movies.

### Auxiliary

तो हल्ली इथे नसतो.  to həlli ithe nəsto.

Nowadays he is not here.

**Colloquial form of imperfect B.** In colloquial speech the form of imperfect B given above is used only for the third person plural. For other numbers and persons, a combination of A and B is generally used. The formula for the underlying form is:

$$N \quad V\text{–}t\text{–}E\text{–}_{imf} \quad Aux$$

In actual speech, however, the auxiliary is partially elided. Note also that the feminine singular ending *e* is raised to *i*. The full paradigm of *ja–*'to go,' is given below.

mi    jatoe
mi    jatie
tu    jatoes
tu    jaties
to    jatoe
ti    jatie
te    jatə:e
amhi  jatoaot
tumhi jatahat
te, tya,  ti jataet

This special colloquial form is limited to the present affirmative.


## 2. The perfect

Action in the perfect is viewed as complete. The formula for the perfect depends on the type of verb.

( 1 ) **Intransitive verbs.** The formula for the perfect with intransitive verbs is:

$$N \quad V{-}l{-}e_{perf} \quad Aux$$

where $E_{perf}$ indicates the set of perfect endings presented in Table 5.8.

Table 5.8.    *Perfect Endings for Intransitive Verbs*

| Person | Singular | | | Plural | | |
|---|---|---|---|---|---|---|
|        | M | F | N | M | F | N |
| 1 | o | e | – | o | o | – |
| 2 | a | i | – | a | a | – |
| 3 | a | i | ə: | e | ya | i |

In speech the present auxiliary is elided. See 4.B.2. for the elided forms.

माझा भाऊ दिल्लीला गेला.          majha bhau dillila gela.
                                  My brother went to Delhi.

माझा भाऊ दिल्लीला गेला आहे.       majha bhau dillila gelae.
                                  My brother has gone to Delhi.

माझा भाऊ दिल्लीला गेला होता.        majha bhau dillila gela hota.
                                    My brother had gone to Delhi.

माझा भाऊ दिल्लीला गेला असेल.        majha bhau dillila gela əsel.
                                    My brother has probably gone
                                    to Delhi.

माझा भाऊ दिल्लीला गेला असणार.       majha bhau dillila gela əsṇar.
                                    My brother has probably gone
                                    to Delhi.

माझा भाऊ दिल्लीला गेला असावा.       majha bhau dillila gela əsava.
                                    My brother has probably gone
                                    to Delhi.

**Meaning.** The verb constructions in the first three sentences above have a meaning similar to that of the past, present perfect and past perfect in English. However, they differ slightly from the English constructions in the range of their use. The first sentence simply declares that the brother went to Delhi, without any reference to whether he has returned or not. The second sentence means that the brother has gone to Delhi recently and has not yet returned. The third sentence means that the brother went and came back; that is, the action is completely finished.

**Perfect without auxiliary.** In addition to the perfect participle + auxiliary construction, there is a form of the perfect without the auxiliary. This construction has the same endings as the construction with the auxiliary, except in the second person, where an *s* is added in the singular and a *t* is optionally added in the plural.

This form is particularly used in the narration of a sequence of events. The first sentence will set the time with the full participle + auxiliary construction. Subsequent sentences will have this modified form.

मी हॉटेलमधे बसलो होतो.          mi hətelmədhe *bəslo hoto*. ek maṇus
एक माणूस आतमधे येऊन            atmədhe yeun majhyajəvəḷ *bəsla*.
माझ्याजवळ बसला. " भयंकर         " bhəyəŋkər ukədtə:e, " mi səhəj
उकडतंय, " मी सहज म्हणालो.       *mhənalo*.

                                I was sitting in a restaurant.
                                A man came in and sat down
                                beside me. " It's terribly hot, "
                                I said casually.

**Auxiliary.** The auxiliary has a perfect form, but it is restricted to complex sentences. See 9.B./4.2 and 9.B.5./1,2 for its use.

( 2 ) **Transitive verbs.** The formula for the perfect with transitive verbs is:

$$N_1\text{--}ni \quad N_2 \quad V\text{--}1\text{--}E_{adj} \quad Aux$$

where $E_{adg}$ represents the regular set of variable adjective endings.

| Singular | | | Plural | | |
|---|---|---|---|---|---|
| M | F | N | M | F | N |
| a | i | ə: | e | ya | i |

The subject $N_1$ is followed by the instrumental postposition *ni.*[*] The verb ending must agree in gender and number with the direct object $N_2$. When the subject is in the second person singular, the main verb agrees with the direct object and the auxiliary agrees with the subject. In all other cases the auxiliary agrees with the direct object.

Normally when a person is a direct object, the noun representing the person is followed by the postposition *la*. This in effect makes the person an indirect object. In this case the ending is neuter singular.

Below is the paradigm of *kər–* ' to do, ' used with the singular direct object *ḳam* and the present auxiliary.[**] Note that all verb constructions are identical, except for the second person singular.

| | |
|---|---|
| मी काम केलं आहे. | mi kam kelə:e. |
| तू काम केलं आहेस. | tu kam kelə:es. |
| त्यानी काम केलं आहे. | tyani kam kelə:e. |
| तिनी काम केलं आहे. | tini kam kelə:e. |
| आम्ही काम केलं आहे. | amhi kam kelə:e. |
| तुम्ही काम केलं आहे. | tumhi kam kelə:e. |
| त्यांनी काम केलं आहे. | tyanni kam kelə:e. |

[*]In formal speech and writing the singular instrumental postposition is *ne* and the plural is *ni.* In the colloquial speech of some persons, the singular is *nə:* and the plural *ni.*

[**]The forms of the pronoun + *ni* are given in Table 3.7. Note that *tyani* represents both *to* + *ni* and *te* ( *n. sg.* ) + *ni*, and *tyanni* represents the third person plural + *ni* for all genders.

In the paradigm above the direct object stayed the same and the subject changed from sentence to sentence. The sentences below illustrate the opposite situation: the subject is the same and the direct object changes.

शेतकऱ्यांनी ज्वारी पेरली आहे।      šetkəryanni ǰvari perlie.
The farmers have planted jowar.

शेतकऱ्यांनी कांदे लावले आहेत।      šetkəryanni kande lavle aet.
The farmers have planted onions.

शेतकऱ्यांनी खूप काम केलं आहे।      šetkəryanni khup kam kelə:e.
The farmers have done a lot of work.

The sentences below illustrate the use of the perfect with other forms of the auxiliary.

शेतकऱ्यांनी ज्वारी पेरली होती।      šetkəryanni ǰvari perli hoti.
The farmers had planted jowar.

शेतकऱ्यांनी ज्वारी पेरली असेल।      šetkəryanni ǰvari perli əsel.
The farmers must have planted jowar.

शेतकऱ्यांनी ज्वारी पेरली असणार।      šetkəryanni ǰvari perli əsṇar.
The farmers must have planted jowar.
The farmers will have planted jowar.

शेतकऱ्यांनी ज्वारी पेरली असावी।      šetkəryanni ǰvari perli əsavi.
The farmers have probably planted jowar.

**Person as direct object**. Below are examples of sentences in which a person is a direct object. Note that the verb ending is in the neuter singular.

मास्तरांनी मुलाला मारलं।      mastəranni mulala marlə:.
The teacher hit the boy.

मी रामला विचारलं आहे।      mi ramla vicarlə:e.
I have asked Ram.

त्यांनी चांगल्या विद्यार्थ्यांना
निवडलं आहे.      tyanni caŋgiya vidyarthyanna nivədlə:e.
They have chosen good students.

Like intransitive verbs, transitive verbs are also used in the perfect without an auxiliary when a sequence of events is being narrated. The narration begun above could be continued:

" तुम्ही कोणच्या गावचे ? "                      "tumhi koṇčya gavce ? " mi tyala
मी त्याला *विचारलं.* पण त्यानी                   *vičarlə:.* pəṇ tyani kahi uttər dilə:
काही उत्तर दिलं नाही.                            nahi.

I asked him, " Where are you from ? "
but he didn't answer.

As in the intransitive, if the subject is in the second person singular, *s* is added
to the verb ending. If the subject is in the second person plural, a *t* is optionally
added.

तू निबंध चांगला लिहिला आहेस.                     tu nibəndhə caŋgla lihila aes.
                                                You have written the essay well.

तुम्ही खूप मदत केलीत.                            tumhi khup mədət kelit.
                                                You helped a lot.

( 3 ) **Special transitive verbs.** Special transitive verbs are a small set of
transitive verbs which like intransitive verbs agree with the subject rather than
the direct object in the perfect. The most common of these are:

| | | |
|---|---|---|
| शिक— | šik— | to learn |
| नेस— | nes— | to put on (a sari) |
| विसर— | visər— | to forget |
| पि— | pi— | to drink |

मी मराठी शिकलो.                                  mi mərathi šiklo.
                                                I learnt Marathi.

ती साडी नेसली.                                   ti saḍi nesli.
                                                She put on a sari.

तो फोन करायला विसरला.                            to fon kərayla visərla.
                                                He forgot to phone.

तो कॉफी प्यायला.                                  to kəfi pyayla.
                                                He drank the coffee.

( 4 ) **N-la impersonal verbs.** The formula for the perfect with *N-la* impersonal
verbs is:

$$N_1\text{-}la \quad N_2 \quad V\text{-}l\text{-}E \quad Aux$$

The ending *E* agrees with $N_2$. The *E* endings are the regular adjective endings

त्यांना माल मिळाला आहे.                          tyanna mal miḷalae.
                                                They have received the goods.

त्यांना माल मिळाला होता.                  tyanna mal milala hota.
                                        They had received the goods.

त्यांना माल मिळाला असेल.                 tyanna mal milala əsel.
                                        They have probably received the
                                        goods.

**Negative**. As with the imperfect, the negative of the perfect is formed by using
the negative auxiliary.

*Intransitive*

तो तिकडे गेला नाही.                       to tikḍe gela nahi.
                                        He hasn't gone there.
                                        He didn't go there.

तो तिकडे गेला नव्हता.                      to tikḍe gela nəvhta.
                                        He hadn't gone there.

तो तिकडे गेला नसेल.                       to tikḍe gela nəsel.
                                        He probably hasn't gone there.

*Transitive*

त्यांनी काम केलं नाही.                     tyani kam kelə: nahi.
                                        He hasn't done the work.
                                        He didn't do the work.

त्यांनी काम केलं नव्हतं.                    tyani kam kelə: nəvhtə:.
                                        He hadn't done the work.

त्यांनी काम केलं नसेल.                     tyani kam kelə: nəsel.
                                        He probably hasn't done the work.

*N–la Impersonal*

त्याला माल मिळाला नाही.                   tyanna mal milala nahi.
                                        They haven't received the goods.

त्यांना माल मिळाला नव्हता.                 tyanna mal milala nəvhta.
                                        They hadn't received the goods.

त्यांना माल मिळाला नसेल.                  tyanna mal milala nəsel.
                                        They probably haven't received
                                        the goods.

## 3. The prospective

Action in the prospective is viewed as about to take place. The formula for the prospective with transitive and intransitive verbs is:

$$N \quad V\text{-}ṇar \quad Aux$$

*Intransitive*

तो आज जाणार आहे.
to aj jaṇar ae.
He is going today.

तो आज जाणार होता.
to aj jaṇar hota.
He was going today.

तो आज जाणार असेल.
to aj jaṇar əsel.
He is probably going today.

*Transitive*

तो आज काम सुरू करणार आहे.
to aj kam suru kərṇar ae.
He is going to begin work today.

तो आज काम सुरू करणार होता.
to aj kam suru kərṇar hota.
He was going to begin work today.

तो आज काम सुरू करणार असेल.
to aj kam suru kərṇar əsel.
He's probably going to begin work today.

*N–la Impersonal*

The formula for the prospective with *N–la* impersonal verbs is:

$$N_1\text{-}la \quad N_2 \quad V\text{-}ṇar \quad Aux$$

where the auxiliary agrees with $N_2$.

आपल्याला माल उद्या मिळणार आहे.
aplyala mal udya miḷṇar ae.
We are going to receive the goods tomorrow.

आपल्याला माल उद्या मिळणार होता.
aplyala mal udya miḷṇar hota.
We were going to receive the goods tomorrow.

Note that the sentences with the past auxiliary imply that something was about to happen, then didn't.

*Auxiliary*

साहेब आता घरी असणार.                        saheb ata ghəri əsṇar.
                                           Saheb is most likely at home now.

सिमल्यात आता थंडी असणार.                   simlyat ata thəṇḍi əsṇar.
                                           It's most likely cold in Simla now.

# Chapter six

# ADJUNCTS OF THE SIMPLE SENTENCE

## A. Adverbs

Adverbs are adjuncts of the simple sentence. As in English, the position of adverbs is less rigidly fixed than that of other elements. Generally, however, an adverb precedes the verb it modifies.

Most adverbs are invariable. A few are variable. These agree in gender and number with the word with which the verb agrees. They use the regular adjective endings.

The majority of adverbs fall into one of four categories: adverbs of time, of extent, of manner, and of place. Some of the most common of these are listed below, with examples of their use.

### 1. Adverbs of time

| | | |
|---|---|---|
| काल | kal | yesterday |
| आज | aj | today |
| उद्या | udya | tomorrow |
| परवा | pərva | day after tomorrow, day before yesterday |
| सकाळी | səkaḷi | in the morning |
| दुपारी | dupari | in the afternoon |
| संध्याकाळी | səndhyakaḷi | in the evening |
| रात्री | ratri | at night |
| पहाटे | pəhaṭe | at dawn |
| आता | ata | now |

| | | |
|---|---|---|
| अगोदर | əgodər | before |
| नंतर | nəntər | afterwards |
| लवकर | ləvkər | soon |
| मग | məg | then |
| ताबड्तोब | tabədtob | immediately |
| लगेच | ləgec | immediately |
| क्वचित | kvəčit | seldom |
| नेहमी | nehemi | always |
| सारखं *(opt. var.)* | sarkhə: | constantly |
| पुष्कळदा | puškəḷda | often |
| अधूनमधून | adhunmədhun | occasionally |
| अजून | əjun | yet, still |
| कधी | kədhi | ever ( used with negative verbs ) |
| नुकतं *(var.)* | nuktə: | a while ago, recently |
| कधी कधी | kədhi kədhi | now and then |
| सहसा | səhəsa | generally ( used with negative verb ) |
| अलिकडे | əlikəḍe | these days, recently |
| रात्रौ | ratrəu | at night ( in announcements of timings of programs ) |
| दिवसा | divsa | during the day |

Strictly speaking, *səkaḷi* and the four words following it are locative forms of the noun. However, they function as adverbs and are treated as such here. Similarly, *ratrəu* and *divsa* are old case forms now functioning as adverbs.

The sentences below give examples of invariable adverbs of time.

| | |
|---|---|
| आज या. | aj ya. Come today. |
| ते काल संध्याकाळी आले. | te kal səndhyakaḷi ale. He came last evening. |
| ते परवा दुपारी दिल्लीला जाणार. मग कलकत्त्याला जाणार. | te pərva dupari dillila jaṇar, məg kəlkəttyala jaṇar. The day after tomorrow in the afternoon he is going to Delhi. Then he is going to Calcutta. |

The sentences below give examples of variable adverbs of time.

| | |
|---|---|
| ते नुकतेच आले. | te nuktec ale. |
| | He came recently. |
| | |
| त्या नुकत्याच आल्या. | tya nuktyac alya. |
| | She came recently. |
| | |
| तो सारखा गप्पा मारीत असतो. | to sarkha gəppa marit əsto. |
| | He's always gabbing. |
| | |
| त्यांनी नुकतंच ते काम संपवलं. | tyanni nuktə:c te kam səmpəvlə:. |
| | He just finished the work a while ago. |

## 2. Adverbs of extent

| | | |
|---|---|---|
| अगदी | əgdi | quite, very, completely |
| जरा | jəra | rather, somewhat |
| फार | phar | very |
| निदान | nidan | at least |
| इतकं ( *opt. var.* ) | itkə: | so much, so |
| खूप | khup | very much, very |

| | |
|---|---|
| आमची परीक्षा फार अवघड होती. | amči pərikša phar avghəḍ hoti. |
| | Our examination was very difficult. |
| | |
| तो इतका हळू बोलतो आहे की मला ऐकू येत नाही. | to itka həḷu boltoe ki məla əiku yet nahi. |
| | He is speaking so softly that I can't make out what he's saying. |

## 3. Adverbs of manner

| | | |
|---|---|---|
| सावकाश | savkaš | slowly |
| हळू | həḷu | with little force or volume |
| भराभर | bhərabhər | rapidly |
| स्पष्ट | spəšťə | clearly, frankly |
| काळजीपूर्वक | kaḷjipurvək | carefully |

| सहज | səhəj | casually, without any particular reason, easily |
| सरळ | sərəḷ | straight |
| सावकाश बोला. | savkaš bola. | |
| | | Please speak slowly. |
| तो फार भराभर बोलतो. | to phar bhərabhər bolto. | |
| | | He speaks very rapidly. |

There are a number of adjectives of manner which have the ending –*un*. These appear to be verb forms with the subordinating conjunction *un* (see 9.B.4.1.), but in some cases they have a meaning slightly different from the original verb. In other cases, the basic verb is not found in the language at all. Some of these words are listed below.

| दरारून | dərarun | profusely |
| ठासून | ṭhasun | ringingly, emphatically |
| जपून | jəpun | carefully |
| निक्षून | nikšun | positively, explicitly |
| हटकून | həṭkun | unfailingly |

## 4. Adverbs of place

| इथे | ithe | here |
| तिथे | tithe | there |
| इकडे | ikḍe | here (with verbs of motion) |
| तिकडे | tikḍe | there (with verbs of motion) |
| सगळीकडे | səgḷikəḍe | everywhere |
| वर, वरती | vər, vərti | above, upstairs |
| खाली | khali | down, below, downstairs |
| जवळ | jəvəḷ | near |
| दूर | dur | far |
| समोर | səmor | in front of |
| शेजारी | šejari | next to |
| आत | at | inside |
| आतमधे | atmədhe | inside |
| बाहेर | baher | out, outside |
| मागे | mage | behind |
| एकत्र | ekətrə | together |

| बरोबर | bərobər | together, along |
|---|---|---|
| लांब | lamb | far |
| अलिकडे | əlikəḍe | this side |
| पलिकडे | pəlikəḍe | that side |

आम्ही तिथे पाच वर्षें राहिलो.   amhi tithe pac vəršə: rahilo.
We stayed there five years.

तुम्हाला खाली बसावं लागेल.   tumhala khali bəsavə: lagel.
You'll have to sit down.

इकडे ये.   ikḍe ye.
Come here.

## 5. Other adverbs

| कदाचित | kədačit | perhaps |
|---|---|---|
| नक्की | nəkki | definitely |
| बहुतेक | bəhutek | probably |
| एकूण | ekuṇ | altogether |
| पैकी | pəiki | among, included in |

## 6. Interrogative adverbs

| कसं | kəsə: ( *var.* ) | how |
|---|---|---|
| केव्हा | kevhā | when |
| कधी | kədhi | when |
| कुठे | kuṭhe | where |
| का | ka | why |

## B.  Postpositions

Postpositions are relational words similar to English prepositions except that they follow rather than precede the word to which they are related. Attached to nouns, pronouns, or verbs, they form phrases that function as adverbs and occupy the same position as adverbs in the sentence.

With the exception of the possessive postposition *cə:*, postpositions are invariable.*

Postpositions fall into three categories: postpositions of place, of time, and of abstract relations.

Following are the most common postpositions, with examples of their use. Those preceded by a hyphen are used only as postpositions. Those without a hyphen are also independent adverbs.

## 1. Postpositions of place

| | | |
|---|---|---|
| आत, –त, –मधे | at, –t, –mədhe | in, inside, between |
| वर | vər | on, to |
| खाली | khali | under |
| –कडे | –kəḍe | to, towards, at the place of |
| –पर्यंत** | –pəryəntə | up to, until |
| जवळ | jəvəḷ | near, with |
| –पाशी | –paši | near, with |
| –ला | –la | to |
| –शी, –स | –ši, –s | to, with (in limited contexts; see examples below) |
| –हून, ऊन | –hun, –un | from |
| अलिकडे | əlikəḍe | on this side |
| पलिकडे | pəlikəḍe | on that side, beyond |
| आसपास | aspas | in the vicinity |
| शेजारी | šejari | next door to |
| समोर | səmor | in front of |
| मागे | mage | behind |
| भोवती | bhovti | around |
| बरोबर | bərobər | with |

*cə: is an exception to the statement that postpositions form adverb phrases. As a possessive postposition, it forms an adjective phrase, and agrees in gender and in number with the noun modified. For examples of its use, see 9.A.1.

**Note that *pəryəntə* refers to both place and time.

## 2. Postpositions of time

| | | |
|---|---|---|
| अगोदर | əgodər | before |
| आधी | adhi | before |
| पूर्वी | purvi | before |
| नंतर | nəntər | after |

## 3. Postpositions of abstract relations

| | | |
|---|---|---|
| नी (ने) (नं) | ni (ne) (nə:) | by, by means of |
| —साठी | —saṭhi | for |
| —हून | —hun | more than |
| —पेक्षा | —pekša | more than |
| —करता | —kərta | for |
| —बद्दल | —bəddəl | about, concerning |
| —प्रमाणे | —prəmaṇe | according to |
| —मुळे | —muḷe | because of |
| —वरून | —vərun | because of |
| —ऐवजी | —əiveji | instead of |

| | | |
|---|---|---|
| तो स्टेशनवर गेला. | to stešənvər gela. | He went to the station. |
| मी रोज त्यांच्याकडे जातो. | mi roj tyančyakəḍe jato. | I go to his place every day. |
| तुम्ही डॉक्टरकडे जा. | tumhi ḍokṭərkəḍe ja. | Go to a doctor. |
| त्या देवळापर्यंत जा. | tya devḷapəryəntə ja. | Go up to that temple. |
| पाचपर्यंत इथे थांबा. | pacpəryəntə ithe thamba. | Stay here until five. |
| त्यांचं घर स्टेशनजवळ आहे. | tyancə: ghər sṭešənjəvəḷ ae. | His house is near the station. |
| तुमच्या जवळ पाच रुपये आहेत का ? | tumčyajəvəḷ pac rupaye aet ka ? | Do you have five rupees with you ?* |

*See 9.A.1 for a discussion of the various ways of expressing possession.

ते देवळापाशी राहतात.                te devḷapaši rahtat.
                                    They live near the temple.

मी ते तुझ्यासाठी आणलं.              mi te tujhyasaṭhi aṇlə:.
                                    I brought it for you.

हे पुस्तक कशाबद्दल आहे ?           he pustək kəšabəddəl ae ?
                                    What is this book about ?

त्यांच्यापाशी काहीच नाही.          tyančyapaši kahic nahi.
                                    They don't have anything.


## 4. Notes

( 1 ) *la* is also used with a personal noun functioning as a direct object.

त्यानी मला सांगितलं.               tyani məla saŋgitlə:.
                                    He told me.

ते चांगल्या विद्यार्थ्यांना निवडतात.   te caŋglya vidyarthyanna nivəḍtat.
                                    They choose good students.

मी मुलांना खो–खो खेळताना पाहिलं.   mi mulanna kho–kho kheḷtana pahilə:.
                                    I saw the children playing kho–kho.

( 2 ) *ši* is used commonly in only a few contexts. It is required with *bol–* ' to speak,' *ləgnə kər–* ' to marry,' and *bhaṇḍ–* ' to quarrel .' Some other senses of 'with' and 'to' also are expressed by *ši*.

मी त्यांच्याशी बोललो.              mi tyančyaši bollo.
                                    I talked to him.

मी पोळी चटणीशी खाल्ली.             mi poḷi cəṭṇiši khalli.
                                    I ate the *poli* with chutney.

माझा त्यांच्याशी काही संबंध नाही.   majha tyančyaši kahi səmbəndhə nahi.
                                    I don't have anything to do with him.
                                    (Lit., ' I don't have any relationship
                                    with him. ')

त्या पेटीशी चाळा करू नकोस.        tya peṭiši caḷa kəru nəkos.
                                    Don't fool with that box.

| | |
|---|---|
| ह्या रेषेशी काटकोन करून रेषा काढ. | hya rešeši kaṭkon kərun reša kaḍh. |
| | Draw a line at right angles to this one. |
| त्यांनी शिंद्यांच्या मुलीशी लग्न केलं. | tyanni šindyancya muliši ləgnə kelə:. |
| | He married Shinde's daughter. |

( 3 ) *un* is often used in combination with a preceding postposition or adverb.

| | |
|---|---|
| तो घरातून बाहेर पडला. | to ghəratun baher pəḍla. |
| | He came out (lit., ' from out of ') the house. |
| ह्यावरून तुम्हाला काय समजतं ? | hyavərun tumhala kay səməjtə: ? |
| | What do you understand from this ? |
| तिकडून आम्ही इथे आलो. | tikḍun amhi ithe alo. |
| | From there we came here. |
| पुण्यापासून सोलापूर किती मैल आहे ? | puṇyapasun solapur kiti məil aə ? |
| | How far is Sholapur from Poona ? |
| तेव्हापासून आमची भेट झाली नाही. | tevhapasun amči bheṭ jhali nahi. |
| | Since then we haven't met. |
| आळंदीपासून पंढरपूरपर्यंत ते चालत जातात. | aḷəndipasun pəndhərpurpəryəntə te caḷət jatat. |
| | They go on foot from Alandi to Pandharpur. |
| एकपासून पन्नासपर्यंत मोजा. | ekpasun pənnaspəryəntə moja. |
| | Count from one to fifty. |
| ते वर्षातून एकदा घरी येतात. | te vəršatun ekda ghəri yetat. |
| | He comes home once a year. |

In colloquial speech *un* is often reduced to *nə:*.

| | |
|---|---|
| घरातून | ghəratun |
| घरातनं | ghəratnə: |
| कडून | kəḍun |
| कडनं | kəḍnə: |

( 4 ) *s* has a limited distribution. It is most commonly used with directions. In colloquial speech it is replaced by *la* even in this context:

| उत्तरेस | uttəres | to the north |
| दक्षिणेस | dəkšiṇes | to the south |

*s* is also used in certain formal verb forms.

| असं करण्यास काही हरकत·नाही. | ʌsə: kərṇyas kahi hərkət nahi. |
| | There is no objection to doing this. |
| सगळ्यांनी एकत्र येऊन प्रयत्न केल्यास परिस्थिती सुधारेल. | səglyanni ekətrə yeun prəyətnə kelyas pəristhiti sudharel. |
| | If everyone comes together and makes an effort, the situation will improve. |

For a discussion of the first construction, see 10.1./2; for the second, see 9.B.5./2.

( 5 ) The instrumental postposition is *ni* in most people's speech. In writing *ne* is used. Some speakers use *nə:* rather than *ni* in the spoken form.

This postposition is used in a variety of ways.

( a ) with the names of tools

| ते हातोड्यानी ठोका. | te hatoḍyani ṭhoka. |
| | Pound it with a hammer. |
| हे त्यानी हातानी बनवलं. | he tyani hatani bənəvlə :. |
| | He made it by hand. |

( b ) with the names of vehicles or routes

| आम्ही विमानानी आलो. | amhi vimanani alo. |
| | We came by plane. |
| आम्ही शिरवळ मार्गानी आलो. | amhi širvəḷ margani alo. |
| | We came by way of Shirval. |

( c ) with nouns referring to time

| थोड्या वेळानी या. | thoḍya veḷani ya. |
| | Come after a short time. |
| आपण खूप दिवसांनी भेटलो. | apəṇ khup divsanni bheṭlo. |
| | We have met after a long time. |

( d ) as an instrumental suffix with transitive verbs in the perfect

रामनी काम केलं.

> ramni kam kelə: .
> Ram worked.

त्या लोकांनी आम्हाला मदत केली.

> tya lokanni amhala mədət keli.
> Those people helped us.

( e ) as an indication of manner

त्यांनी जोरानी ब्रेक लावला.

> tyanni jorani brek lavla.
> He stepped hard on the brake.

तो शांतपणाने तिथे बसला होता.

> to šantəpənane tithe bəsla hota.
> He was calmly seated there.

( f ) in the sense ' in terms of '

तो वयानी लहान आहे.

> to vəyani ləhan ae,
> He is young (lit., ' small in age').

तो अंगानी मोठा आहे.

> to aŋgani moṭha ae.
> He is big (lit., ' big in body').


4. Expressions of time

There are four different constructions for expressions of time. Compare the following sentences.

मी पाच वर्षे तिथे राहिलो.

> mi pac varšə: tithe rahilo.
> I stayed there for five years.

माझा भाऊ दोन वर्षांनी परत आला.

> majha bhau don vəršanni pərət ala.
> My brother came back after two years.

त्यांनी दोन महिन्यांत हे घर बांधलं.

> tyanni don məhinyat he ghər bandhlə:.
> They built this house in two months.

मी महिन्यातून एकदा इथे येतो.

> mi məhinyatun ekda ithe yeto.
> I come here once a month.

Note that in the first sentence the time expression *pac vərsə:* is used without a postposition. This has the meaning ' for a period of.' The second sentence uses the postposition *ni*. This construction has the sense 'after a period of.'

In the third sentence the postposition *at* is used. This means 'within a period.' In the final sentence the combined form *atun* is used. This form is used for expressions of frequency.


## C.   Particles

Particles differ from postpositions in that they are attached to the straight form of the noun rather than the oblique. They may also be attached to other parts of speech. The most common particles in Marathi are *c* and *hi*.

### 1.   *c.*

*c* is an emphatic particle. It singles out and emphasizes the word it is attached to.

तेच पाहिजे.                          tec pahije.
                                     That's the one I want.

त्यांनीच ते केलं.                      tyannic te kelə:
                                     He's the one who did it.

दोनच द्या.                           donəc dya.
                                     Give two (no more, no less).

जूनमध्ये पाऊस पडतोच.                  junmədhe paus pədtoc.
                                     It definitely rains in June.

आम्ही जायला निघालो               amhi jayla nighalo tevḍhyat
तेवढ्यात तो आलाच.                   to alac.

                                     He came just as we were leaving.

मला ते आजच पाहिजे.                 məla te ajəc pahije.
                                     I want it *today*.

ती जातेच आहे तर मंडईतून           ti jatec ae tər məṇḍəitun bhaji aṇil.
भाजी आणील.                         Since she's going anyway, she will
                                     bring some vegetables from the market.

2. *hi*

*hi* means ' also. '

| | |
|---|---|
| तेही येणार आहेत. | tehi yeṇar aet.<br>They are coming too. |
| मी त्यांनाही ती गोष्ट सांगितली. | mi tyannahi ti goṣṭə saŋgitli.<br>I told the story to him too. |
| तिथेही हवा थंड असते. | tithehi həva thəṇḍə əste.<br>The weather is cold there too. |

*hi* also serves as an intensifier of meaning, especially to heighten contrast.

| | |
|---|---|
| मला त्याच्याबद्दल काहीही माहीत नाही. | məla tyačyabəddəl kahihi mahit nahi.<br>I don't know anything at all about that. |
| तुम्ही कुठेही गेला तरी तेच सापडणार. | tumhi kuṭhehi gela təri tec sapəḍnar.<br>No matter where you go, that's what you'll find. |
| गेल्या वर्षापेक्षाही आता किमती जास्त आहेत. | gelya vəršapekšahi ata kimti ȷ̆astə aet.<br>Prices are now even higher than last year. |

# Chapter seven

# OPERATORS

## A. Verb Operators

There are certain elements that can be added to the verbal root to alter the meaning. These may be called verb operators.

1. *–ayla lag–*        begin to V

तो काम करायला लागतो.        to kam kərayla lagto.
He begins to work.

तो काम करायला लागला.        to kam kərayla lagla.
He began to work.

तो काम करायला लागेल.        to kam kərayla lagel.
He will begin to work.

मला मराठी समजायला लागलं आहे.        məla mərathi semjayla laglə:e.
I have begun to understand Marathi.

मला शास्त्रीय संगीत आवडायला
लागलं आहे.        məla šastriyə saŋgit avḍayla laglə:e.
I have begun to like classical music.

2. *–u lag–*        begin to V

This construction has the same meaning as *–ayla lag–* but is more formal.

तो बोलू लागतो.        to bolu lagto.
He begins to speak.

तो बोलू लागला.        to bolu lagla.
He began to speak.

114

तो बोलू लागेल.
to bolu lagel.
He will begin to speak.

त्याला इंग्रजी समजू लागलं आहे.
tyala iŋgrəʲi səmju laglə:e.
He has begun to understand English.

3. *–t bəs–* to go on V–ing

This construction, like its English counterpart, often contains an implied criticism.

तो गप्पा मारीत बसतो.
to gəppa marit bəsto.
He goes on chatting.

तो गप्पा मारीत बसला.
to gəppa marit bəsla.
He went on chatting.

4. *–t rah–* to go on V–ing

Unlike *–t bəs–* this implies no criticism.

दिवसभर पाऊस पडत राहिला.
divəsbhər paus pədət rahila.
It went on raining all day long.

महिनाभर झाडांना पालवी येत राहते.
məhinabhər jhaḍanna palvi yet rahte.
The trees keep getting new leaves for a month.

आज दिवसभर फोन बाजत राहणार.
aj divəsbhər fon vajət rahnar.
The phone is going to be ringing all day today.

5. *–t al–* have been V–ing

मी आजपर्यंत हेच करीत आलो आहे.
mi ajpəryəntə hec kərit aloe.
I have always been doing this.

तो गेली दहा वर्षे मुंबईला दर बुधवारी जात आला आहे.
to geli dəha vəršə: mumbəila dər budhvari jat alae.
For the last ten years he has been going to Bombay every Wednesday.

तो नेहमीच आपलं काम वेळेवर करीत आला आहे.
to nehemic aplə: kam veḷevər kərit alae.
He has always done his work on time.

With verbs having the sense of 'to be completed,' 'to be used up,' or 'to come to maturity,' this construction means 'is nearly V–ed.'

| | |
|---|---|
| साखर संपत आली आहे. | sakhər səmpət alie. |
| | The sugar is nearly finished. |
| भात शिजत आला आहे. | bhat šijət alae. |
| | The rice is nearly done. |
| पाणी आटत आलं आहे. | paṇi aṭət aləːe. |
| | The water is almost dried up. |
| आंबे पिकत आले आहेत. | ambe pikət ale aet. |
| | The mangoes are nearly ripe. |
| सतरंजी फाटत आली आहे. | sətrənji phaṭət alie. |
| | The carpet has almost worn out. |
| काम होत आलं आहे. | kam hot aləːe. |
| | The work is almost done. |

6.  –u sək–                              to be able to V

This construction is less used than  N–la V–ta ye–.

| | |
|---|---|
| मी केव्हाही येऊ शकतो. | mi kevhahi yeu šəkto. |
| | I can come at any time. |
| तो काल येऊ शकला नाही. | to kal yeu šəkla nahi. |
| | He couldn't come yesterday. |
| तो उद्या येऊ शकेल. | to udya yeu šəkel. |
| | He will be able to come tomorrow. |

7.  V₁–un V₂                             Compound verb

Many verbs can be used in this special compound form. The second verb is one of a small set of verbs used with attenuated meaning. Consider the following examples.

| | |
|---|---|
| हे काम लवकर संपवून टाका. | he kam ləvkər səmpvun ṭaka. |
| | Finish up this work quickly. |
| मी लगेच उत्तर लिहून टाकलं. | mi ləgec uttər lihun ṭakləː. |
| | I wrote off an answer immediately. |
| बघून घ्या. | bəghun ghya. |
| | Have a look. |

| | |
|---|---|
| लिहून घ्या. | lihun ghya. |
| | Write it down (for yourself). |
| लिहून द्या. | lihun dya. |
| | Write it down (for me). |
| मी ते सगळं फेकून दिलं. | mi te səgḷə: phekun dilə:. |
| | I threw it all away. |

In each of these examples, the second verb — *ṭak-*, *ghe-*, *de-* — has only a vestige of its normal meaning. It primarily serves as an intensifier of the meaning of the first verb. Compare this usage with that of the prepositions *up* and *off* with English verbs: 'Write up the story,' 'Send off the letter.' The verb *ṭak-* is generally used in regard to finishing an activity, *ghe-* in regard to doing something directed towards oneself, and *de-* in regard to doing something directed away from oneself. This construction is highly idiomatic and only experience will enable one to use it with assurance.

The resultant construction $V_1$-*un* $V_2$ appears identical with the construction joining two actions in a series with the conjunction *V—un*. This compound construction is probably derived from the binary construction, but is no longer identical with it and should not be confused with it.

8.  *—t ja*                 continue to V

This can be used only with the imperative.

| | |
|---|---|
| आमच्याकडे येत जा. | amčyakəḍe yet ja. |
| | Come over now and then. |
| असं करीत जा. | əsə: kərit ja. |
| | Keep on doing this. |

9.  *—u pah—*               to try to V

This construction implies effort in spite of some obstacle.

| | |
|---|---|
| लोक कार्यक्रमात घुसू पहात होते. | lok karyəkrəmat ghusu pəhat hote. |
| | People were trying to push their way into the program. |
| पक्ष्यांनी उडू पाहिलं. | pəkšyanni uḍu pahilə:. |
| | The birds tried to fly. |

## B.  Sentence Operators

There is a fairly small set of sentences that can be used as a frame for almost any sentence or question. The most common of these are listed below. In the formulas *S* stands for the reported sentence.

1. (a)  *N (əsə:) əik–  ki S*          N  hear–  that S
       *mhən–*                    say–
       *vicar–*                   ask–

मी असं ऐकलं की त्यांची मीटिंग          mi əsə: əiklə: ki tyanči miʈiŋg
उद्या होणार आहे.                      udya honar ae.
                                            I heard that their meeting
                                            was going to take place tomorrow.

ते म्हणाले की उद्या आम्ही इकडे येऊ.          te mhənale ki udya amhi ikɖe yeu.
                                            They said that they would come here
                                            tomorrow.

त्यांनी मला (असं) विचारलं          tyaᴜnni məla (əsə:) vičarlə:
(की) तू कुठे जातो आहेस.          (ki) tu kuʈhe jatoes.
                                            He asked me where I was going.

त्यांनी मला (असं) विचारलं          tyanni məla (əsə:) vičarlə:
(की) तू जाणार आहेस का.          (ki) tu janar aes ka.
                                            He asked me if I was going.

Note that unlike English, reported speech in Marathi does not require an indirect construction. Following *ki* the actual words of the speaker are given, without the change of pronoun or tense required in English.

The above patterns can be shifted around so that the reported sentence comes first, with the pattern

   ( b )  *S  əsə:  N  əik–*
                *mhən–*
                *vicar–*

त्यांची मीटिंग उद्या होणार          tyanči miʈiŋg udya honar ae
आहे असं मी ऐकलं.          əsə: mi əiklə:.

आम्ही उद्या तिकडे येऊ असं          amhi udya tikɖə: yeu əsə: te
ते म्हणाले.          mhənale.

तू कुठे जातो आहेस असं
त्यांनी मला विचारलं.

tu kuṭhe jatoes əsə: tyanni
məla viček arlə:.

तू जाणार आहेस का असं
त्यांनी मला विचारलं.

tu jaṇar əes ka əsə: tyanni
məla viček arlə:.

2. $N_1$ $N_2$-la (əsə:) saŋg- ki S      $N_1$ tell- $N_2$ that S

त्यांनी आम्हाला असं सांगितलं
की यंदा पीक फार चांगलं आहे.

tyanni amhala əsə: saŋgitlə:
ki yənda pik phar caŋglə: ae.

He told us that the crop is very
good this year.

3. (a) N-la mahit Aux ki S      N know- that S

मला माहीत आहे की पगार
फार कमी आहे.

məla mahit ae ki pəgar phar
kəmi ae.

I know that the pay is very low.

(b) S te N-la mahit Aux
      he

पगार फार कमी आहे ते
मला माहीत आहे.

pəgar phar kəmi ae te məla
mahit ae.

4. (a) (N-la) (əsə:) vaṭ- ki S      N feel- that S
             kəḷ-              N find- out that S
             dis-             It appear- that S

मला (असं) वाटतं की हिंदीपेक्षा
मराठी अवघड आहे.

məla (əsə:) vaṭṭə: ki hindipekša
maraṭhi əvghəḍ ae.

I feel that Marathi is more
difficult than Hindi.

मला असं कळलं की सगळी
माहिती इथेच मिळेल.

məla əsə: kəḷḷə: ki səgḷi
mahiti ithec miḷel.

I learned that all the information
could be obtained right here.

असं दिसतं की पुढच्या वर्षी
परिस्थिती सुधारेल.

əsə: distə: ki puḍhčya vərši
pəristhiti sudharel.

It looks as if the situation will
improve next year.

( b ) S *əsə: (N–la) vaṭ–*
                         *kəl–*
                         *dis–*

हिंदीपेक्षा मराठी अवघड आहे
असं मला बाटतं.

हिंदिपेक्षा मराठी अवघड आहे
असं मला बाटतं.

səgḷi mahiti ithec miḷel əsə:
məla kəḷḷə:.

पुढच्या वर्षी परिस्थिती सुधारेल
असं दिसतं.

puḍhčya vərši pəristhiti sudharel
əsə: distə:.

सगळी माहिती इथेच मिळेल
असं मला कळलं.

हिंदीपेक्षा मराठी अवघड आहे means at left... 

5. ( a ) *N–ci əši khatri Aux ki S*        N is confident that S
                   *kəlpəna*               N has the idea that S

माझी अशी खात्री आहे की          majhi əši khatri ae ki tyala cəŋglə:
त्याला चांगलं काम करता येईल.     kam kərta yeil.

                                          I am confident that he will be able to
                                          do a good job.

( b ) S *əši N–ci khatri Aux*

त्याला चांगलं काम करता येईल      tyala cəŋglə: kam kərta yeil əši
अशी माझी खात्री आहे.            majhi khatri ae.

6. ( a ) *N–la kəlpəna Aux ki S**         N has the inkling that S

आम्हाला कल्पना नव्हती की         amhala kəlpəna nəvhti ki itke lok
इतके लोक येतील.                 yetil.

                                          We had no idea that so  many people
                                          would come.

( b ) S *hyaci kəlpəna N–la  Aux*

इतके लोक येतील त्याची           itke lok yetil hyači kəlpəna
कल्पना आम्हाला नव्हती.          amhala nəvhti.

7. ( a ) *N–cya (əsə:) ləksat ye– ki S*   N realize– that S
                   *mənat*                It come– into N's mind that S

---

*Note the difference between the two uses of *kəlpəna* ' idea.' *N–la kəlpəna*
*Aux* means ' N has an inkling that,' while *N–ci əši kəlpəna Aux* means ' N has
the idea ( notion ) that. '

माझ्या लक्षात असं आलं की ह्या
बाबतीत मला काहीच करता येत नव्हतं.

majhya ləkšat (əsə:) alə: ki hya
babtit məla kahic kərta yet nəvhtə:.

I realized  that  in  this  matter there
was nothing I could do.

त्याच्या मनात ( असं ) आलं की
आपण मुंबईत नोकरी शोधावी.

tyačya mənat (əsə:) alə: ki apəṇ
mumbəit nokri šodhavi.

He felt that he should  look for a job
in Bombay.

( b ) *S  əsə:  N–cya  ləksat ye-*
　　　　　　　　*mənat*

ह्या बाबतीत मला काहीच करता येत
नव्हतं असं माझ्या लक्षात आलं.

hya babtit məla kahic kərta yət
nəvhtə: əsə: majhya ləkšat alə:.

आपण मुंबईत नोकरी शोधावी असं
त्याच्या मनात आलं.

apəṇ mumbəit nokri šodhavi əsə:
tyačya mənat alə:.

# Chapter eight

# UNARY TRANSFORMATIONS

## A. Basic Patterns

Simple sentences may be modified by certain operations, which we may call unary transformations. Below are listed some of the most important unary transformations in Marathi.

It will be noted that many of these constructions have similar meanings, especially those dealing with necessity and obligation. Though we have tried to indicate the distinct meaning of each construction, it should be kept in mind that in actual use the constructions are often interchangeable.

### 1. *V–ayc–E  Aux**

( 1 ) Any *N  V* sentence in which N is a person can be transformed into *N–la  V–ayc–E  Aux*. The meaning of this construction is ' N wants to V ' or ' N is to V.' The ending is the regular adjective ending; it agrees with the direct object.** If there is no direct object, it is neuter singular.

---

*In these formulas, unless specifically mentioned otherwise, *V* may be either transitive or intransitive. In order to simplify the formulas, the object of the transitive verb has not been shown.

**Throughout this chapter the term ' direct object ' has been used somewhat loosely. Strictly speaking, it is debatable whether $N_2$ should be termed a direct object in sentences like $N_1$–*la*  $N_2$  *V–aycə: ae* or $N_1$–*ni*  $N_2$  *V–ayla, pahije*. However, for simplicity of expression, we have used ' direct object to refer to $N_2$ in such constructions.

| त्याला काम करायचं आहे. | tyala kam kərayco:e. |
| | He wants to work. |
| | He is to work. |
| | He has work to do. |

| त्याला काम करायचं होतं. | tyala kam kərayco: hotə:. |
| | He wanted to work. |
| | He was to work. |
| | He had work ¦to do. |

| त्याला काम करायचं असेल. | tyala kam kərayco: əsel. |
| | He probably wants to work. |
| | He probably is to work. |
| | He probably has work to do. |

| त्याला काम करायचं नाही. | tyala kam kərayco: nahi. |
| | He doesn't want to work. |

| त्याला काम करायचं नाही आहे. | tyala kam kərayco: naie. |
| | He doesn't want to work. |
| | He doesn't have work to do. |

( 2 ) *N–ni* may be substituted for *N–la* in construction 1.

The meaning of this construction is 'N should V,' 'N is the one who should V,' or 'N is to V.' The agreement rules are the same as in 1.

Like construction 1 above, this construction can also be used with the auxiliary in the past or future. To avoid repetition, examples with the past and future auxiliaries have not been included here.

| त्यानी हे काम करायचं आहे. | tyani he kam kərayco:e. |
| | He should do this work. |

| त्यानी तिथे जायचं आहे. | tyani tithe jayco:e. |
| | He should go there. |

## 2. *V–ayla pahĭje (Aux)*

( 1 ) Any *N V* sentence in which the subject is a person can be transformed into *N–la V–ayla pahije (Aux)* 'N has to V.' Note that in the formula *Aux* in given in parentheses, indicating that it may be deleted. However, deletion is permissible only for the present auxiliary, not the past or future.

Rules for agreement depend on whether or not there is a direct object and whether or not the auxiliary is used. If there is no direct object and the auxiliary is not used, *pahije* remains unchanged. If there is no direct object and the auxiliary is used, *pahije* remains unchanged and the ending of the auxiliary is neuter singular. If there is a direct object and the auxiliary is used, *pahije* remains unchanged and the auxiliary has the regular adjective endings agreeing with the direct object. If there is a direct object and no auxiliary is used, *pahije* agrees with the direct object in number, remaining unchanged if the direct object is singular and adding a *t* if the direct object is plural.

मला मुंबईला जायला पाहिजे. (आहे.)    məla mumbəila jayla pahije (ae).

I have to go to Bombay.

मला आंबे तोडायला पाहिजे आहेत.    məla ambe toḍayla pahije aet.
मला आंबे तोडायला पाहिजेत.    məla ambe toḍayla pahijet.

I have to pick the mangoes.

गेल्या महिन्यात त्याला दिल्लीला    gelya məhinyat tyala dillila jayla
जायला पाहिजे होतं.    pahije hotə:.

Last month he should have gone
to Delhi.
Last month he wanted to go
to Delhi.

( 2 ) In construction (1) *N–ni* may be substituted for *N–la*. The meaning then becomes ' should V ' rather than ' has to V. '

त्यांनी दिल्लीला जायला पाहिजे.    tyanni dillila jayla pahije.
He should go to Delhi.

त्यांनी दिल्लीला जायला पाहिजे होतं.    tyanni dillila jayla pahije hotə:.
He should have gone to Delhi.*

*Note the difference in meaning when the past auxiliary is used. The basic sense of *pahije* implies something yet to be fulfilled. Thus in the sentence above the implication is that he never got to Delhi.

### 3. *V–l–E pahije*

( 1 ) Any *N V* sentence in which the subject is a person can be transformed into *N–ni V–l–E pahije* 'N must V.' This construction expresses greater necessity than *N–la V–ayla pahije*.

*E* is the regular adjective ending. It agrees with the direct object. If there is no direct object, *E* is neuter singular. *pahije* also agrees with the direct object, adding a *t* if the direct object is plural.

| | |
|---|---|
| त्यानी गेलं पाहिजे. | tyani gelə: pahĭje. |
| | He must go. |
| त्यानी काम केलं पाहिजे. | tyani kam kelə: pahĭje. |
| | He must work. |
| त्यानी गाडी दुरुस्त केली पाहिजे. | tyani gaḍi durustə keli pahĭje. |
| | He must repair the car. |
| त्यानी गाड्या दुरुस्त केल्या पाहिजेत. | tyani gaḍya durustə kelya pahĭjet. |
| | He must repair the cars. |

( 2 ) In the above construction *N–la* may be substituted for *N–ni* with little change of meaning.

| | |
|---|---|
| त्याला काम केलं पाहिजे. | tyala kam kelə: pahĭje. |
| | He must work. |
| त्याला गेलं पाहिजे. | tyala gelə: pahĭje. |
| | He must go. |

4. Any *N V* sentence in which the subject is a person can be transformed into *N–la V–av–E lag– (Aux)* ' (for N) to have to V.' This is apparently somewhat stronger than *N–ni V–l–E pahije*.

| | |
|---|---|
| मला जावं लागतं. | məla javə: lagtə:. |
| | I have to go ( habitually ). |
| मला जावं लागलं ( होतं ). | məla javə: laglə: ( hotə: ). |
| | I had to go. |
| मला जावं लागणार. | məla javə: lagṇar. |
| | I am going to have to go. |
| मला जावं लागेल. | məla javə: lagel. |
| | I will have to go. |

मला काम करावं लागतं.

məla kam kəravə: lagtə:.
I have to work ( habitually ).

मला काम करावं लागलं (होतं).

məla kam kəravə: laglə: (hotə:).
I had to work.

मला काम करावं लागणार.

məla kam kəravə: lagṇar.
I am going to have to work.

मला काम करावं लागेल.

məla kam kəravə: lagel.
I will have to work.

If there is a direct object, the ending *E* agrees with it; otherwise it is neuter singular.

त्याला पुष्कळ गोष्टी बघाव्या लागतात.

tyala puškəḷ gošṭi bəghavya lagtat.
He has to see to a lot of things.

5. Any *N V* sentence in which the subject is a person can be transformed into *N-la V-ta ye-* 'N is able to V.'

मला जाता येतं.

məla jata yetə:.
I can go.

मला जाता आलं.

məla jata alə:.
I was able to go.

मला मराठी बोलता येतं.

məla mərathi bolta yetə:.
I can speak Marathi.

मला मराठी बोलता येत नव्हतं.

məla mərathi bolta yet nəvhtə:.
I didn't use to be able to speak Marathi.

6. Any *N V* sentence in which the subject is a person can be transformed into *N-ni V-ta kama nəye* 'N ought not to V.'

त्यानी असं करता कामा नये.

tyani əsə: kərta kama nəye.
He ought not to do this.

त्यानी तिथे जाता कामा नये.

tyani tithe jata kama nəye.
He ought not to go there.

7. Any *N V* sentence in which *N* is a person can be transformed into *N-la V-ayla avəd-* 'N likes to V.'

त्याला पोहायला आवडतं.     tyala pohayla avədtə:.
He likes to swim.

त्यांना सिनेमाला जायला आवडतं.     tyanna sinemala jayla avədtə:.
They like to go to the movies.

8. Any $N_1 V_1$ sentence can be transformed into $N_2 N_1 V_1$-*u de*- '(for) $N_2$ to let $N_1 V_1$.'

भात शिजू द्या.     bhat šiju dya.
Let the rice cook.

आम्ही त्याला खेळू दिलं.     amhi tyala kheḷu dilə:.
We let him play.

The imperative form of this construction has an invariant alternant:
*N V–u det* 'Let N V.'

त्याला ते करू देत.     tyala te kəru det.
Let him do it.

त्याला येऊ देत.     tyala yeu det.
Let him come.

9. A sentence $N_1 N_2 V$ can be transformed into $N_3 N_1$-*kəḍun* $N_2 V$–*un ghe*- 'for $N_3$ to have $N_2$ V–ed by $N_1$.'*

मी शिंप्याकडून पोलकं शिवून घेतलं.     mi šimpyakəḍun polkə: šivun ghetlə:.
I had the blouse stitched by the tailor.

तो सुताराकडून कपाट करून घेणार आहे.     to sutarakəḍun kəpaṭ kərun gheṇar ae.
He is going to have the cupboard made by the carpenter.

10. **Passive.** Any sentence of the form $N_1 N_2 V$ can be transformed into the passive construction ( $N_1$-*kəḍun* ) $N_2 V$–*l–E ja*– 'for $N_2$ to be V–ed ( by $N_1$ ).' As in English, the passive is generally used when the agent is not to be stressed, so the phrase designating the agent ( *N–kəḍun* ) is usually not used. The ending *E* is the regular adjective ending, agreeing with $N_2$.

---

*This was probably originally a causative form *V–əvun* ( see 11.D.2 ). If it is thought of as a causative, the meaning is more readily understandable.

| | |
|---|---|
| भारतामधे पुष्कळ भाषा बोलल्या जातात. | bharətaməddhe pukškə̣ḷ bhaša bollya jatat. |
| | Many languages are spoken in India. |
| सरकारकडून प्रतिनिधी नेमले जातात. | sərkarkəḍun prətinidhi nemle jatat. |
| | The representatives are appointed by the government. |

11. **Another passive construction.**   Any sentence of the form  $N_1$   $N_2$   $V$  can be transformed into another passive construction:  $(N_1- kəḍun/atun)$   $N_2$   $V-ṇyat$   $ye-$.[*]  This construction is particularly used in newspaper reports.

| | |
|---|---|
| अधिकृत गोटातून असं सांगण्यात आलं की... | ədhikrit goṭatun əsə: saŋgṇyat alə: ki... |
| | It was said by an authoritative source that... |
| एक महिन्याने परीक्षेचा निकाल जाहीर करण्यात येईल. | ek məhinyane pərikšeca nikal jahir kərṇyat yeil. |
| | In a month the result of the examination will be announced. |

12. Any  $N$   $V$  sentence may be transformed into:  $N$   $V-lyasivay$   $rah-$   $Aux-_{neg}$  ' for N to V without fail. '

| | |
|---|---|
| रोज देवळात गेल्याशिबाय तो रहात नाही. | roj devḷat gelyašivay to rəhat nahi. |
| | He goes to the temple without fail every day. |
| आई त्याला किती रागवली तरी तो मित्रांकडे गेल्याशिवाय राहिला नाही. | ai tyala kiti ragəvli təri to mitraŋkəḍe gelyašivay rahila nahi. |
| | No matter how angry his mother got at him, he didn't fail to go to his friends. |
| मी शेतीचं उत्पादन वाढवल्याशिबाय राहणार नाही. | mi šeticə: utpadən vaḍhəvlyašivay rahṇar nahi. |
| | I will not fail to increase agricultural production. |

[*]The oblique line indicates that *atun* is an alternant of *kəḍun*.

**13. Pluperfect.** Any sentence of the form *N(–ni) V–l–E Aux* (that is, any sentence in the perfect ) can be transformed into the pluperfect *N(–ni) V–lel–E Aux*. Like the English past perfect, this form indicates that an action was relatively further back in the past. The normal rules for agreement in the perfect govern the ending *E*.

मी त्याच्याकडे गेलो त्यावेळी तो बाहेर गेलेला होता.
mi tyaȼyakǝḍe gelo tyaveḷi to baher gelela hota.

When I went to his place he had gone out.

हा खेळ मी पुष्कळदा खेळलेलो आहे.
ha kheḷ mi puškǝḷda kheḷleloe.

I have often played this game.

**14.** Any *N V* sentence can be transformed into *N(–ni) V–lel–E bǝr–E* ' It would be best if N V–ed. ' The form of the ending *E* depends on whether *V* is transitive or intransitive and on which person *N* is.

( a ) If *V* is transitive the endings follow the normal rules for the perfect with transitive verbs.

( b ) If *V* is intransitive and *N* is in the first or second person, the endings are in the neuter singular. This means in effect that *N* is in the instrumental form.

( c ) If *V* is intransitive and *N* is in the third person, there are two options.

( i ) *N* may be in the subject form and the *E* endings in agreement with it.

( ii ) *N* may be in the instrumental and the *E* endings neuter singular.

आपण हा भात संपवून टाकलेला बरा.
apǝṇ ha bhat sǝmpvun ṭaklela bǝra.
We'd better finish up this rice.

आम्ही लवकर निघालेलं बरं.
amhi lǝvkǝr nighalelǝ: bǝrǝ:.
We'd better leave soon.

हा आमच्याबरोबर आलेला बरा.
ha amȼyabǝrobǝr alelå bǝra.
He'd better come with us.

यानी आमच्याबरोबर आलेलं बरं.
yani amȼyabǝrobǝr alelǝ: bǝrǝ:.
He'd better come with us.

**15.** *cal–t–E ho–.* In the older stages of the language there was apparently a general rule that a sentence *N V–l–E* (that is, a sentence in the perfect) could be transformed into *N   V–ta ho–*. This transformation is no longer generally applicable, but it does apply to the verb *cal–* ' to walk. '

| ती चालती झाली. | ti calti jhali. |
| | She left. |

| चालता हो. | calta ho. |
| | Get out. |

## B.   Questions

Questions are a type of unary  transformation.  However,  because of their importance they are given here in  a  separate section. Questions are basically of two kinds: yes–no questions, and questions asking for more  information. Within the category of yes–no questions there are  two  sub–types that call  for special attention: rhetorical questions and question tags.

### 1. Yes–no questions

Yes–no questions are formed by adding *ka* to the statement.

| ही तुमची मुलगी आहे. | hi tumči mulgi ae. |
| | This is your daughter. |

| ही तुमची मुलगी आहे का ? | hi tumči mulgi ae ka ? |
| | Is this your daughter *?* |

| त्यांना यायचं आहे. | tyanna yaycɔːe. |
| | He wants to come. |

| त्यांना यायचं आहे का? | tyanna yaycɔːe ka ? |
| | Does he want to come ? |

### 2. Questions asking for more information

These questions are formed by putting the interrogative  word  in the  position in which the desired information will appear in the answer.

| ते कुठे गेले ? | te kuṭhe gele ? |
| | Where did they go ? |

ते कोल्हापूरला गेले.

te kolhapurla gele.
He went to Kolhapur.

त्याला किती अंडी पाहिजेत?

tyala kiti əṇḍi pahiJet ?
How many eggs does he want ?

त्याला चार अंडी पाहिजेत.

tyala čar əṇḍi pahijet.
He wants four eggs.

ते किती वाजता निघणार आहेत ?

te kiti vajta nighṇar aet ?
What time are they starting out ?

ते तीन वाजता निघणार आहेत.

te tin vajta nighṇar aet.
They're starting out at three o'clock.

## 3. Rhetorical questions

Sometimes a question is used purely for rhetorical effect. That is, the speaker is not asking for information; he is making a statement in the form of a question. For example, he may say, " Isn't it hot today ? " when what he means is, " It's very hot today. " Marathi has special forms for at least two kinds of rhetorical questions.

( 1 ) *N thod–E–c V.* For a rhetorical question intended to suggest a negative answer, the form is *N thoḍ–E–c V.* The ending *E* is the regular adjective ending. In sentences with intransitive verbs *E* agrees with the subject. In sentences with transitive verbs it may agree with either the subject or the object.

तो थोडाच तुझं ऐकणार आहे ?

to thoḍac tujhə: əikṇar ae ?
Is he going to listen to you ?
(He is not going to listen to you.)

मी थोडाच त्याच्यावर विश्वास
ठेवणार आहे ?

mi thoḍac tyačyavər višvas
thevṇar ae ?

Am I going to trust him ?
(I am not going to trust him.)

त्या थोडयाच (थोडंच) गाणं
म्हणणार आहेत ?

tya thoḍyac (thoḍə:c) gaṇə:
mhəṇṇar aet ?

Are they going to sing a song ?
(They are not going to sing a song. )

( 2 )  *N bər–E  V.*  For a rhetorical question intended to suggest ' why should  N V ? ' the form is  *N  bər–E  V.*  The ending *E* is the regular adjective ending, and agrees with  *N.*

| | |
|---|---|
| तो बरा येईल ? | to bəra yeil ? |
| | Why should he come ? |
| | |
| मी बरी करीन ? | mi bəri kərin ? |
| | Why should I do it ? |

## 4.  Question tags

As in  English,  a question  tag  may  be  added  to  any  statement.  The question tags are *nahi ka*, *ho ki nahi*, *ho na*, and *na*.

| | |
|---|---|
| ती येणार आहे, नाही का ? | ti yeṇar ae, nahi ka ? |
| | She is going to come, isn't she ? |
| | |
| तू येणार आहेस, नाही का ? | tu yeṇar aes, nahi ka ? |
| | You are going to come,  aren't  you ? |
| | |
| त्यांनी चांगलं काम केलं आहे, नाही का ? | tyanni caŋglə: kam kelə:e, nahi ka ? |
| | They have done good work, haven't they ? |
| | |
| पुस्तकं फार महाग आहेत, नाही का ? | pustəkə: phar məhag aet, nahi ka ? |
| | Books are very expensive,  aren't they ? |
| | |
| तू तिथे गेला होतास, हो की नाही ? | tu tithe gela hotas, ho ki nahi ? |
| | You went there, didn't you ? |
| | |
| तुला नाटक आवडलं, हो ना ? | tula natək avədlə:, ho na ? |
| | You liked the play, didn't you ? |
| | |
| तो आजारी नाही ना ? | to ajari nahi na ? |
| | He isn't sick, is he ? |
| | |
| तू जाणार आहेस ना ? | tu jaṇar ahes na ? |
| | You're going, aren't you ? |
| | |
| त्यानी ते केलं नाही ना ? | tyani te kelə: nahi na ? |
| | He didn't do that, did he ? |

## C. Appositives

A noun in any position may have another noun in apposition to it. Some of the common patterns of apposition are presented below.

(a) common noun + proper noun

हा माझा भाऊ वामन.  ha majha bhau vamən.
This is my brother Vaman.

माझा भाऊ वामन काल आला.  majha bhau vamən kal ala.
My brother Vaman came yesterday.

(b) proper noun + pronoun + common noun

अकबरानी बांधलेलं फत्तेपूर सिक्री हे  əkbərani bandhlelə: phəttepur
शहर आम्ही पाहिलं.  sikri he šəhər amhi pahilə:.*

We saw Fatehpur Sikri, the city built
by Akbar.

(c) In formal speech and in writing it is common to use a pronoun after a proper noun.

अध्यक्ष सर्जेराव भोसले ह्यांनी  ədhykšə sərjerao bhosle hyanni
उद्घाटन केले.  udghaṭən kele.

President Sarjerao Bhosle performed
the opening ceremony.

(d) Similarly, in a formal salutation in a letter the addressee's name is followed by a pronoun.

श्री अनंतराव देशपांडे ह्यांना  šri ənəntrao dešpaṇḍe hyanna
to Shri Anantrao Deshpande

(e) A common noun may also be followed by a pronoun.

मातृत्व हे मंगल असतं.  matṛitvə he məŋgəl əstə:.
Motherhood is sacred.

(f) Place names are sometimes followed by the adverb *yethe* 'here.' This usage is especially common in news reports.

*For the construction *V–lel–E N*, see 9.A.5.

नागपूर येथे विधानसभेचे
अधिवेशन सुरू झाले आहे.

nagpur yethe vidhansəbhece
ədhiveśən suru jhale ae.

The session of the legislative
assembly has started in Nagpur.

# Chapter nine

# BINARY TRANSFORMATIONS

Transformations of two or more sentences into a single sentence are binary transformations.

## A.  Sentences into Noun Phrases

A number of binary transformations are used to change sentences into noun phrases which then can be embedded into another sentence.

**1. Possessive.**  In English the verb ' to have ' is used to express both intrinsic relations and possession of things. That is, we can say ' I have a brother, ' ' A cow has horns, ' and ' I have a pencil. '  In Marathi there is one construction for the first two senses of ' to have, ' and a different construction for the last.

( 1 ) Intrinsic relations are expressed by the construction

| $N_1$–la $N_2$ Aux | $N_1$ has $N_2$ |
|---|---|
| मला भाऊ आहे. | məla bhau ae.<br>I have a brother. |
| रामला दोन भाऊ आहेत. | ramla don bhau aet.<br>Ram has two brothers. |
| तिला दोन मुलं आहेत. | tila don mulə: aet.<br>She has two children. |
| गाईला शिंगं आहेत. | gaila šiŋgə: aet.<br>A cow has horns. |

The possessive transformation changes this sentence into a noun phrase, according to the formula

$$N_1 - poss.\ N_2$$

where *poss.* stands for the possessive. The form of the possessive depends on $N_1$ and $N_2$. If $N_1$ is a noun, the possessive particle *cə:* is used and the ending is the regular adjective ending agreeing with $N_2$ in gender and number. If $N_1$ is a pronoun, the possessive adjective is used, the ending again agreeing with $N_2$ in gender and number.

Thus the sentences above will become:

| | |
|---|---|
| माझा भाऊ | majha bhau<br>my brother |
| रामचे दोन भाऊ | ramce don bhau<br>Ram's two brothers |
| तिची दोन मुलं | tiči don mulə:<br>her two children |
| गाईची शिंगं | gaiči šiŋgə:<br>the cow's horns |

The same transformation may be repeated over and over to make an elaborate noun phrase. For example, the first phrase above can be combined with more phrases.

| | |
|---|---|
| माझा भाऊ | majha bhau<br>my brother |
| माझ्या भावाला मुलगी आहे. | majhya bhavala mulgi ae.<br>My brother has a daughter. |
| माझ्या भावाची मुलगी | majhya bhavači mulgi<br>my brother's daughter |
| माझ्या भावाच्या मुलीला नवरा आहे. | majhya bhavačya mulila nəvra ae.<br>My brother's daughter has a husband. |
| माझ्या भावाच्या मुलीचा नवरा | majhya bhavačya mulica nəvra<br>my brother's daughter's husband |

( 2 ) Ownership of things is expressed by:

$$N_1-\check{c}yaj\partial v\partial \underset{\smile}{l} \quad N_2 \; Aux \qquad N_1 \; \text{has} \; N_2$$
$$pas\check{i}$$
$$k\partial \d{d}e$$

| | |
|---|---|
| त्याच्याजवळ पुस्तकं आहेत. | tyǎčyaj∂v∂ḷ pust∂k∂: aet. |
| | He has some books. |
| त्याच्याकडे पैसे आहेत. | tyǎčyak∂ḍe p∂ise aet. |
| | He has money. |
| तुझ्यापाशी पंचवीस पैसे आहेत का ? | tujhyapaši p∂n̆čvis p∂ise aet ka ? |
| | Do you have twenty–five paise ? |

The above sentences can be transformed:

| | |
|---|---|
| त्याची पुस्तकं | tyǎči pust∂k∂: |
| | his books |
| त्याचे पैसे | tyace p∂ise |
| | his money |
| तुझे पंचवीस पैसे | tujhe p∂n̆čvis p∂ise |
| | your twenty–five paise |

2.  A pair of sentences of the form below may be combined to produce a noun phrase.

$$\begin{aligned} N & \quad Aux \\ N-c\partial: & \; nav \; X \end{aligned} \quad \rightarrow \quad X \; navac\partial: \; N$$

$$\begin{aligned} & \text{There is an N} \\ & \text{N's name is X} \end{aligned} \quad \rightarrow \quad \text{an N named X}$$

| | |
|---|---|
| एक मुलगी आहे. | ek mulgi ae. |
| | There is a girl. |
| तिचं नाव सुमन. | tic∂: nav sum∂n. |
| | Her name is Suman. |
| सुमन नावाची मुलगी | sum∂n navači mulgi |
| | a girl named Suman |
| एक नाटक आहे. | ek naṭ∂k ae. |
| | There is a play. |
| त्याचं नाव " गारंबीचा बापू. " | tyac∂: nav " gar∂mbica bapu. " |
| | It is called " Garambica Bapu. " |

"गारंबीचा बापू" नावाचं नाटक    " garəmbica bapu " navacə: natək
                              a play called " Garambica Bapu "

3. An *N A Aux* sentence can be transformed into the phrase *A N*.

घर मोठं आहे.                   ghər mothə: ae.
                              The house is big.

मोठं घर                        mothə: ghər
                              big house

गाडी चांगली आहे.                gaḍi caŋgli ae.
                              The car is nice.

चांगली गाडी                     caŋgli gaḍi
                              a nice car

4. A sentence of the form below can be transformed into a noun phrase.

$N_1$  $N_2$-at Aux $\rightarrow$ $N_2$ -at- l-E $N_1$
    mədhe      mədh–

                    $N_1$ is in $N_2$ $\rightarrow$ the $N_1$ in $N_2$

*E* is the regular adjective ending agreeing with $N_1$.

त्या कपाटात भांडी आहेत.          tya kəpaṭat bhaṇḍi aet.
                              The pots are in that cupboard.

त्या कपाटातली भांडी              tya kəpaṭatli bhaṇḍi
                              the pots in that cupboard

शाळेमधे मुलं आहेत.               šaḷemədhe mulə: aet.
                              There are children in the school.

शाळेमधली मुलं                    šaḷemədhli mulə:
                              the children in the school

There is a formal variant of this transformation.

$N_1$  $N_2$-at Aux $\rightarrow$ $N_2$ -atil $N_1$
    mədhe      mədhil

                    $N_1$ is in $N_2$ $\rightarrow$ the $N_1$ in $N_2$

The terminations *atil* and *mədhil* are invariant.

त्या देशात लोक आहेत.             tya dešat lok aet.
                              There are people in that country.

त्या देशातील लोक        tya dešatil lok

the people of that country

5. A sentence in the imperfect A may be transformed into a noun phrase.

$$N_1 \ (N_2) \ V\text{-}t\text{-}E_{imf} \ \rightarrow \ (N_2) \ V\text{-}ṇar\text{-}E \ N_1$$

$$N_1 \ V \ (N_2) \ \rightarrow \ \text{the} \ N_1 \ V\text{-}ing \ (N_2)$$

The ending $E$ is the regular adjective ending agreeing with $N_1$.

लोक तिकडे काम करतात.      lok tikḍe kam kərtat.

People work there.

तिकडे काम करणारे लोक      tikḍe kam kərṇare lok

the people working there

बाई कपडे धुते.      bai kəpḍe dhute.

The woman washes clothes.

कपडे धुणारी बाई      kəpḍe dhuṇari bai

the woman who washes clothes

6. A sentence in the imperfect B may be transformed into a noun phrase.

$$N_1 \ (N_2) \ V\text{-}t \ Aux \ \rightarrow \ (N_2) \ V\text{-}t \ əslel\text{-}E \ N_1$$

$$N_1 \ be\text{-} \ V\text{-}ing \ (N_2) \ \rightarrow \ \text{the} \ N_1 \ V\text{-}ing \ (N_2)$$

विकास होत आहे.      vikas hot ae.

Development is taking place.

होत असलेला विकास      hot əslela vikas

the development taking place

देश धान्याची निर्यात करीत आहेत.      deš dhanyači niryat kərit aet.

Countries are exporting grain.

धान्याची निर्यात करीत असलेले देश      dhanyači niryat kərit əslele deš

the countries exporting grain

This construction is formal and rather stilted, however. In speech construction 5, $V\text{-}ṇar\text{-}E \ N$ is commonly used as a transformation of imperfect B as well as imperfect A.

होणारा विकास      hoṇara vikas

the development taking place

धान्याची निर्यात करणारे देश      dhanyači niryat kərṇare deš

the countries exporting grain

7.    A sentence in the imperfect B containing a transitive verb may also be transformed into a phrase with $N_2$, the direct object, as headword.

ते संशोधन करीत आहेत.                    te sə̄všodhən kərit aet.
                                        They are doing research.

ते करीत असलेलं संशोधन                   te kərit əslelə: sə̄všodhən
                                        the research they are doing

8.    ( 1 ) A perfect sentence with  an  intransitive verb may transformed into a noun phrase.

N  V–l–E  →    V–lel–E  N

                                        N  V–ed  →   the  N  who  V–ed

मुलगा तिथे बसला आहे.                    mulga tithe bəslae.
                                        The boy is seated there.

तिथे बसलेला मुलगा                       tithe bəslela mulga
                                        the boy who is seated there

मुलं झोपली आहेत.                        mulə: jhopliet.
                                        The children have  gone to sleep.

झोपलेली मुलं                            jhopleli mulə:
                                        the children who have gone to sleep

( 2 ) A perfect  sentence  with  a transitive verb  may  be transformed  into a noun phrase:

$N_1$–ni  $N_2$  V–l–E    →    $N_1$–ni V–le l–E  $N_2$
                              $N_1$  V–ed  $N_2$   →   the  $N_2$  V–ed  by  $N_1$

त्यानी पुस्तकं घेतली.                   tyani pustəkə: ghetli.
                                        He got the books.

त्यानी घेतलेली पुस्तकं                  tyani ghetleli pustəkə:
                                        the books he got

त्या लोकांनी काम केलं.                  tya lokanni kam kelə:.
                                        Those people did the work.

त्या लोकांनी केलेलं काम                 tya lokanni kelelə: kam
                                        the work those people did

9.    A sentence of the form below can be transformed into a noun phrase.

$$N_1 \ N_2\text{-}pasun \ b\partial n\partial vlel\text{-}E \ Aux \ \rightarrow \ N_2\text{-}poss. \ N_1$$

$$N_1 \ \text{is made from} \ N_2 \ \rightarrow \ N_1 \ N_2$$

With some $N_2$ the following construction also can be used.

$$N_2\text{-}i \ N_1 \qquad\qquad N_2 \ N_1$$

ते टेबल लाकडापासून बनवलेलं आहे.

te ţebǝl lakḍapasun bǝnǝvlelǝ:e.
That table is made of wood.

लाकडाचं टेबल

lakḍacǝ: ţebǝl
a wooden table

लाकडी टेबल

lakḍi ţebǝl
a wooden table

ती भांडी पितळेपासून बनवलेली आहेत.

ti bhaṇḍi pitǝḷepasun bǝnǝvleli aet.
Those vessels are made of brass.

पितळेची भांडी

pitǝḷeči bhaṇḍi
brass vessels

( The option *pitǝḷi bhaṇḍi* is not acceptable. )

10.   *V–t–E N* and *V–l–E N*. There are some noun phrases of the form *V–t–E N* and *V–l–E N*. These are obviously transforms of a simple sentence, but the transformations applied to them are not generally applicable. The interesting thing about these constructions is that the *N* in the transformed sentence is not necessarily the subject of the original sentence; in some cases it is the object of a postposition. In both these constructions *E* is the regular adjective ending, agreeing with *N*.

त्याचं राहतं घर नाशिकला आहे.

tyacǝ: rahtǝ: ghǝr nǎšikla ae.
His residence is in Nasik.

वाहत्या गंगेत हात धुवून घ्यावेत.

vahtya gǝŋget hat dhuvun ghyavet.

One should take the opportunity that presents itself. ( Lit., ' One should wash one's hands in the flowing Ganges.' )

त्यानी पेट्ट्या आगीत उडी घेतली.

tyani peţţya agit uḍi ghetli.
He jumped into the blazing fire.

वाढल्या वयात मुलांना दुधाची गरज        vaḍhtya vəyat mulanna dudhači
असते.                                   gərəj əste.

                                        Growing children need milk.

भरल्या पोटी झोपू नये.                   bhərlya poṭi jhopu nəye.

                                        One should not sleep on a full
                                        stomach.

तिनी त्याला भरल्या गळ्यानी निरोप        tini tyala bhərlya gəḷyani nirop dila.
दिला.                                   Her throat choked with tears, she said
                                        goodbye to him.

## B.   Joining Sentences with Conjunctions

### 1.  Coordinating conjunctions

A pair of simple sentences may be joined by coordinating conjunctions, according to the formula $S_1$ *conj.* $S_2$. The coordinating conjunctions are given below.

| | | |
|---|---|---|
| आणि | aṇi | and |
| की | ki | or |
| किंवा | kĩva | or |
| ना ... ना | na ... na | neither ... nor |
| पण | pəṇ | but |
| परंतु | pərəntu | but |
| म्हणून | mhəṇun | so |
| कारण | karəṇ | because |

( 1 )  *aṇi*

ते सगळ्या मुलांना तपासणार आहेत.    te səgḷya mulanna təpasṇar aet.

                                    They are going to examine all the
                                    children.

ते आजारी मुलांना औषध देणार आहेत.   te ajari mulanna əuṡə̃dh deṇar aet.

                                    They are going to give medicine to the
                                    sick children.

ते सगळ्या मुलांना तपासणार आहेत आणि आजारी मुलांना औषध देणार आहेत.

te səglya mulanna təpasṇar aet aṇi ajari mulanna əuṣ̌ədh deṇar aet.

They are going to examine all the children and give medicine to the sick children.

राम आणि सुरेश येणार आहेत.

ram aṇi sureš yeṇar aet.

Ram and Suresh are going to come.

मला केळी आणि आंबे घ्यायचे आहेत.

məla keḷi aṇi ambe ghyayce aet.

I want to get bananas and mangoes.

मला हे नको आणि तेही नको.

məla he nəko aṇi tehi nəko.

I don't want either this or that.

## (2) *ki, kiva, na...na*

There is some difference in the use of the two words meaning ' or.' *ki* apparently is used when there is an exclusive choice—that is, either A or B, but not both. *kiva*, on the other hand, is used when both A and B are possible.

मी पोळी करू का ?

mi poḷi kəru ka ?

Shall I make poli ?

मी भाकरी करू का ?

mi bhakri kəru ka ?

Shall I make bhakri ?

मी पोळी की भाकरी करू ?

mi poḷi ki bhakri kəru ?

Shall I make poli or bhakri ?

तू येणार आहेस की नाहीस ?

tu yeṇar aes ki nahis ?

Are you going to come or not ?

पैसे मनीऑर्डरनी किंवा चेकनी पाठवा.

pəise məniərḍərni kiva čekni paṭhva.

You may send the money either by money order or by check.

ते मुंबईला किंवा पुण्याला मिळेल.

te mumbəila kiva puṇyala miḷel.

You can get it either in Bombay or in Poona.

*na...na* functions almost exactly as its English counterpart.

त्याला बुद्धी नाही.

tyala buddhi nahi.

He doesn't have brains.

त्याला पैसा नाही.

tyala paisa nahi.

He doesn't have money.

त्याला ना बुद्धी ना पैसा.

tyala na buddhi na pəisa.

He has neither brains nor money.

(3) *pəṇ, pərəntu*

मी त्यांच्याशी बोललो.

mi tyančyaši bollo.

I spoke to him.

त्यांना पटलं नाही.

tyanna pəṭlə: nahi.

He wasn't convinced.

मी त्यांच्याशी बोललो पण
त्यांना पटलं नाही.

mi tyančyaši bollo pəṇ tyanna
pəṭlə: nahi.

I spoke to him but he wasn't
convinced.

लोकसंख्येच्या वाढीवर नियंत्रण केले
पाहिजे हे सगळ्यांना मान्य आहे,
परंतु ते कसे करता येईल त्याबद्दल
मतभेद आहेत.

loksəŋkhyečya vaḍhivər niyəntrəṇ
kele pahiⁱe he səgḷyanna manyə ae,
pərəntu te kəse kərta yeil tyabəddəl
mətəbhed aet.

Everyone agrees that the population
growth should be controlled, but
there are differences of opinion about
how it can be done.

(4) *mhəṇun, karəṇ*

ट्रॅक्टर बिघडला होता.

ṭrækṭər bighəḍla hota.

The tractor went out of order.

काम झालं नाही.

kam jhalə: nahi.

The work didn't get done.

ट्रॅक्टर बिघडला होता म्हणून
काम झालं नाही.

ṭrækṭər bighəḍla hota mhəṇun
kam jhalə: nahi.

The tractor went out of order, so the
work didn't get done.

Note that the same sentences appear in reverse order with *karən*.

| | |
|---|---|
| काम झालं नाही कारण ट्रॅक्टर बिघडला होता. | kam jhalə: nahi karən ṭrækṭər bighəḍla hota. |
| | The work didn't get done because the tractor was out of order. |

## 2. Conjunctive adverbs and postpositional phrases

There are a number of adverbs and postpositional phrases which are used as conjunctions between sentences. In intonation the sentences remain separate. The resulting construction is $S_1$ *conj* $S_2$.

Following are some of the most common conjunctive adverbs and postpositional phrases.

| | | |
|---|---|---|
| तरीपण | təripəṇ | but still, nevertheless |
| तरीसुद्धा | tərisuddha | ,, |
| तरीदेखील | təridekhil | ,, |
| तथापि | təthapi | nevertheless |
| त्यावेळेला | tyaveḷela* | at that time |
| त्यानंतर | tyanəntər | after that |
| त्याअगोदर | tya–agodər | before that |
| त्यापूर्वी | tyapurvi | previous to that |
| त्याच्याआधी | tyačya–adhi** | before that |
| तोपर्यंत | topəryəntə | until then |
| त्यामुळे | tyamuḷe | because of that |
| त्याशिवाय | tyašivay | besides that, without that |
| शिवाय | šivay | besides |
| त्याऐवजी | tyaəivə̆ji | instead of that |
| नाही तर | nahi tər | otherwise |
| त्यासाठी | tyasaṭhi | for that |
| त्याकरता | tyakərta | for that |

*A variant of *tyaveḷela* is *tyaveḷi*.
**In all these phrases *tya* and *tyačya* are interchangeable before a postposition.

त्यांनी खूप प्रयत्न केला तरीपण
त्यांना जमलं नाही.

tyanni khup prəyətnə kela, təripəṇ
tyanna jəmlə: nahi.

He tried very hard; still he couldn't
manage it.

मी एक्रूणसत्तर साली इथे आलो
त्यावेळेला मला मराठी समजत नव्हतं.

mi ekuṇsəttər sali ithe alo tyaveḷela
məla mərathi səmjət nəvhtə:.

I came here in ' 69; at that time I
couldn't understand Marathi.

त्यांचा माल फार महाग असतो.
शिवाय त्याची क्वॉलिटी इतकी
चांगली नसते.

tyanca mal phar məhag əsto.
šivay tyači kvɔliṭi itki cəŋgli
nəste.

Their goods are very expensive;
besides the quality is not very good.

## 3. Relative constructions

( 1 ) A pair of sentences joined so that the second sentence refers to some element of the first is called a *relative construction*. In Marathi, the first clause is introduced by an element beginning with *j*, the second by an element beginning with *t*. Following are the relative forms.

| जो | तो | jo | to | he, that |
|---|---|---|---|---|
| जेव्हा | तेव्हा | jevhā | tevhā | when |
| जसं | तसं | jəsə: | təsə: | just as, in the same way |
| जितकं | तितकं | jitkə: | titkə: | as much as |
| जेवढं | तेवढं | jevḍhə: | tevḍhə; | as much as |
| जिथे | तिथे | jithe | tithe | where |
| जिकडे | तिकडे | jikḍe | tikḍe | where |

Unless the *j* element has an ending different from the *t* element, the first may be omitted.

आज सकाळी (जो) तुमच्याबरोबर
आला होता तो कोण आहे ?

aj səkaḷi (jo) tumčyabərobər
ala hota to koṇ ae ?

Who was that who came with you
this morning ?

काल ज्यानी गाणं ग्हटलं त्याचं नाव काय ?

kal j̈yani gaṇə: mhəṭlə: tyacə: nav kay ?

What is the name of the man who sang a song yesterday ?

(जेव्हा) तुम्ही कोल्हापूरला जाल तेव्हा त्यांच्याकडे जाऊन भेटा.

(j̈evhā) tumhi kolhapurla jal tevhā tyanc̈yakəde jaun bheṭa.

When you go to Kolhapur go and meet him.

(जितकी) पाहिजेत तितकी पुस्तकं घ्या.

(jitki) pahijet titki pustəkə: ghya.

Take as many books as you like.

( 2 ) *jo to* when used together as a single subject means ' each person ' or ' everybody. '

जो तो आपल्या कामात मग्न होता.

jo to aplya kamat məgnə hota.

Everyone was absorbed in his own work.

ज्यानी त्यानी आपलं पाहवं.

j̈yani tyani aplə: pəhavə:.

Each one should look after his own affairs.

ज्यानी त्यानी उठून सरकारवर टीका केल्याने काहीच साध्य होत नाही.

j̈yani tyani uṭhun sərkarvər ṭika kelyane kahic sadhyə hot nahi.

Nothing is accomplished if everybody just gets up and criticizes the government.

( 3 ) The doubled form of the relative pronouns: *jo jo to to* is used to mean ' the more ... the more. ' This construction is fairly uncommon. It is apparently used only in situations involving repeated action.

जो जो पुसे तो तो चिकटे.

jo jo puse to to čikṭe.

The more he wiped it the more it stuck.

( 4 ) *mhənje* often functions as a copulative verb. It is also used, however, in a relative construction: $S_1$ *mhənje* $S_2$ ' When $S_1$ then $S_2$.'

गाडी आली म्हणजे मी जाईन.

gaḍi ali mhəṇ̇je mi jain.
When the car comes I will go.

पगार मिळाला म्हणजे मी साड्या
खरेदी करीन.

pəgar miḷala mhəṇ̇je mi saḍya khəredi
kərin.
When I get my salary I will buy some
saris.

( 5 ) *ki* is also used in a relative construction: $S_1$ *ki* $S_2$ ' When $S_1$ then $S_2$. '

एप्रिल महिना आला की उकडायला
लागतं.

epril məhina ala ki ukḍayla
lagtə:.
When April comes it starts to get
hot.

पाऊस पडला की ओढ्यांना
पाणी येतं.

paus pədla ki oḍhyanna paṇi
yetə:.
When it rains the streams flow.

( 6 ) *to* is also used in a relative construction: $S_1$ *to* $S_2$ ' When $N_1$ $V_1$ $N_2$ $V_2$. '
Note that in these sentences the imperfect A is used for a past event. If *toc* is
used the meaning is ' as soon as. '

आम्ही तिथे जातो तो
सगळं संपून गेलेलं होतं

amhi tithe jato to səgḷə:
səmpun gelelə: hotə:.
When we arrived there
everything was already finished.

आम्ही स्टेशनवर पोचतो तोच
तिची गाडी आली.

amhi sṭešənvər pocto toc tiči
gadi ali.
As soon as we arrived at the station,
her train arrived.

( 7 ) There are a few fixed expressions of the form $N_1$ *to* $N_2$ *aṇi* *V*, meaning
' Not only is $N_1$ $N_2$ but also $N_1$ *V*. ' This construction is practically obsolete.

चोर तो चोर आणि वर शिरजोर.

cor to cor aṇi vər širjor.
Not only is he a thief but he is
headstrong to boot.

मिकारडी ती भिकारडी आणि
सांगितलेलं ऐकत नाहीस.

bhikarḍi ti bhikarḍi aṇi
saŋgitlelə: əikət ṇahis.

Not only are you a beggar but you
don't listen to what you are told.

This second example is taken from *sukrəvarci kəhaṇi*. Note that it is in the second person, but the third person pronoun *ti* is used in the first clause.

## 4. Subordinating conjunctions

Following are the transformations employing subordinating conjunctions to make a sentence into a dependent clause.

(1) *V–un.* A pair of sentences of the form below may be combined into a single sentence.

$$
\begin{array}{l}
N_1 \quad V_1 \\
(məg) \; N_1 \quad V_2
\end{array}
\rightarrow N_1 \quad V_1\text{–}un \quad V_2
$$

$$
\begin{array}{l}
N_1 \quad V_1 \\
\text{Then} \quad N_1 \quad V_2
\end{array}
\rightarrow N_1 \quad V_1 \quad \text{and} \quad V_2
$$

The resultant sentence may also have the form

$$V_1\text{–}un \quad N_1 \quad V_2$$

मी तिकडे जातो.

mi tikḍe jato.
I go there.

मी त्याला भेटतो.

mi tyala bheṭto.
I meet him.

मी तिकडे जाऊन त्याला भेटतो.

mi tikḍe jaun tyala bheṭto.
I go there and meet him.

तो घरी आला.

to ghəri ala.
He came home.

तो जेवायला बसला.

to jevayla bəsla
He sat down to eat.

तो घरी येऊन जेवायला बसला.

to ghəri yeun jevayla bəsla.
He came home and sat down to eat.

| त्यानी पुस्तक हातात घेतलं. | tyani pustək hatat ghetlə:.<br>He took the book in his hand. |
| तो वाचायला लागला. | to vacayla lagla.<br>He began to read. |
| पुस्तक हातात घेऊन तो वाचायला लागला. | pustək hatat gheun to vacayla lagla.<br>He took the book in his hand and began to read. |

Note that if one verb is transitive and one intransitive, the form of the subject is determined by $V_2$.

Compound verb constructions look like the *V–un* transformation, but are derived differently. For a discussion of compound verb constructions, see 7.A.7.

( 2 ) *V–lya* + *post.* A pair of sentences of the form below may be combined into a single sentence.

$$N_1 \ V_1$$
$$tyanəntər \ N_{(2)}^* \ V_2 \quad \longrightarrow \quad N_1 \ V_1\text{-}lyanəntər \ N_{(2)} \ V_2$$

$$N_1 \ V_1$$
$$\text{After that } N_{(2)} \ V_2 \quad \longrightarrow \quad \text{After } N_1 \ V_1, \ N_{(2)} \ V_2$$

In place of *nəntər* the following postpositions may be used.

| वर | vər | after, on |
| बरोबर | bərobər | immediately after |
| मुळे | muḷe | because of |
| शिवाय | šivay | without, unless |
| कारणानी | karṇani | because of |
| ने | ne | by, on account of, because of |

| तो तिकडे गेला. | to tikḍe gela.<br>He has gone there. |
| त्यानंतर तो काय करणार ? | tyanəntər to kay kərṇar ?<br>What is he going to do ? |

*The parentheses around 2 indicate that the *N* may be a repetition of $N_1$ ( that is, that the subject of both sentences may be the same ) or may be a different *N* ( that is, that the second sentence has a different subject ).

तिकडे गेल्यानंतर तो काय करणार ?

tikḍe gelyanəntər to kay kərṇar?

After going there what is he going to do ?

तू बी. ए. होशील.

tu bi e hošil.

You will get your B. A.

मग तू काय करणार ?

məg tu kay kərṇar?

Then what will you do ?

बी. ए. झाल्यावर तू काय करणार ?

bi e jhalyavər tu kay kərṇar?

What will you do after you get your B. A. ?

तो घरी आला.

to ghəri ala.

He came home.

लगेच तो झोपायला गेला.

ləgec to jhopayla gela.

He went to bed.

घरी आल्याबरोबर तो झोपायला गेला.

ghəri alyabərobər to jhopayla gela.

As soon as he got home, he went to bed.

त्यानी आम्हाला मदत केली.

tyani amhala mədət keli.

He helped us.

त्यामुळे आम्हाला काही त्रास झाला नाही.

tyamuḷe amhala kahi tras jhala nahi.

Because of that, we didn't have any difficulty.

त्यानी आम्हाला मदत केल्यामुळे आम्हाला काही त्रास झाला नाही.

tyani amhala mədət kelyamuḷe amhala kahi tras jhala nahi.

Because he helped us, we didn't have any difficulty.

खत वापरायला पाहिजे.

khət vaprayla pahije.

One must use fertilizer.

नाही तर धान्याचं चांगलं उत्पन्न
येत नाही.

nahi tər dhanyacə: caŋglə: utpənnə
yet nahi.

Otherwise one doesn't get a good
yield of grain.

खत वापरल्याशिवाय धान्याचं
चांगलं उत्पन्न येत नाही.

khət vapərlyašivay dhanyacə:
caŋglə: utpənnə yet nahi.

Unless one uses ( without using )
fertilizer, one doesn't get a good
yield of grain.

शिक्षकांचा संप आहे.

šikšəkanca səmpə ae.
There is a teachers' strike.

म्हणून आज शाळा बंद आहे.

mhəṇun aj šaḷa bəndə ae.
Because of that school is closed
today.

शिक्षकांचा संप असल्याकारणाने
आज शाळा बंद आहे.

šikšəkanca səmpə əslyakarṇane
aj šaḷa bəndə ae.

Because there is a teachers' strike
school is closed today.

आपण भरभर चढण चढतो.

apən bhərbhər cəḍhəŋ cəḍhto.
We climb a slope rapidly.

म्हणून आपल्याला दम लागतो.

mhəṇun aplyala dəm lagto.
On account of that we get tired.

चढण भरभर चढल्याने आपल्याला
दम लागतो.

cəḍhəŋ bhərbhər cəḍhlyane
aplyala dəm lagto.

We get tired from climbing a
slope rapidly.

( 3 ) *V–lya V–lya*. The construction $N_1$ $V_1$*–lya* $V_1$*–lya* $N_{(2)}$ $V_2$ means
' Just as ( as soon as ) $N_1$ $V_1$–ed, $N_{(2)}$ $V_2$–ed ' or ' while $N_1$ $V_1$–ed $N_{(2)}$
$V_{(2)}$–ed.' This construction is fairly uncommon, and cannot be used freely to
construct new sentences.

मी बाहेर निघाल्या निघाल्या  
पावसाला सुरवात झाली.

mi baher nighalya nighalya  
pavsala survat jhali.

Just as I went outside, it started  
to rain.

तिकडे गेल्या गेल्या त्याला निरोप दे.

tikḍe gelya gelya tyala nirop de.

Give him the message as soon as  
you get there.

मी बसल्या बसल्या ते पुस्तक वाचून  
संपवलं.

mi bəslya bəslya te pustək vacun  
səmpəvlə:.

I finished the book at one sitting.

मी पडल्या पडल्या विचार करीत होते.

mi pəḍlya pəḍlya vičar kərit hote.

As I was lying there I was thinking.

The form *ghərbəslya* ' while sitting at home ' is related to the above construction.

टी व्ही मुळे घरबसल्या आम्हाला  
क्रिकेट मॅच बघायला मिळाली.

ṭi vhimuḷe ghərbəslya amhala  
krikeṭ mæč bəghayla miḷali.

Because of TV we got to watch the  
cricket match while sitting at home.

( 4 ) *V–l–E* *nə*: *V–l–E*. The construction $N$ $V_1$–$l$–$E$ *nə*: $V_1$–$l$–$E$ *to* $S$ means ' No sooner does N V than S. ' The ending $E$ follows the normal rules for agreement in the perfect. This construction, like its English counterpart, is fairly uncommon.

सहा वाजले न वाजले तो देवळात  
भजनाला सुरवात होते.

səha vajle nə: vajle to devḷat  
bhəjənala survat hote.

No sooner does it strike six than the  
bhajan starts in the temple.

( 5 ) *V–lya* *nə*: *V–lyasarkh–E*. The construction $N$–*ni* $V_1$–*lya* *nə*: $V_1$–*lyasarkh–E* *kel–E* means ' N V–ed but acted as if he hadn't. ' The ending $E$ follows the normal rules for agreement in the perfect. This construction is fairly uncommon.

मला पाहिल्या न पाहिल्यासारखं
करून तो ओळख न दाखवता
निघून गेला.

məla pahilya nə: pahilyasarkhə:
kərun to oḷəkh nə: dakhəvta
nighun gela.

Acting as if he hadn't seen me and
without showing that he recognized
me, he went on.

( 6 ) *V–i–pəryəntə (V–i–stəvər).* A pair of sentences of the form below
may be combined into a single sentence. Note that the verb in the first sentence
is in the future.

$$N_1 \quad V_1{-}i{-}E_f$$
$$topəryəntə \;\; N_{(2)} \;\; V_2 \quad \rightarrow \quad N_1 \quad V{-}i{-}pəryəntə \;\; N_{(2)} \;\; V_2$$

$$N_1 \;\; \text{will} \;\; V_1$$
$$\text{Until then} \;\; N_{(2)} \;\; V_2 \quad \rightarrow \quad \text{Until} \;\; N_1 \;\; V_2 \;\; N_{(2)} \;\; V_2$$

तो येईल.

to yeil.
He will come.

तोपर्यंत मी थांबेन.

topəryəntə mi thamben.
Until then I will wait.

तो येईपर्यंत मी थांबेन.

to yeipəryəntə mi thamben.
I will wait until he comes.

तो जागा होईल.

to jaga hoil.
He will wake up.

तोपर्यंत तू बाहेर जाऊ नकोस.

topəryəntə tu baher jau nəkos.
Until then don't go outside.

तो जागा होईपर्यंत तू बाहेर
जाऊ नकोस.

to jaga hoipəryəntə tu baher
jau nəkos.
Until he wakes up, don't go outside.

( 7 ) *V–tana.* A pair of sentences in the imperfect B, that is, of the form
below, may be combined into a single sentence.

$$N_1 \;\; V_1{-}t \;\; Aux$$
$$tyavelela \;\; N_{(2)} \;\; V_2{-}t \;\; Aux \quad \rightarrow \quad N_1 \;\; V_1{-}tana \;\; N_{(2)} \;\; V_2{-}t \;\; Aux$$

$$N_1 \;\; \text{is} \;\; V_1{-}ing$$
$$\text{At that time} \;\; N_{(2)} \;\; \text{is} \;\; V_2{-}ing \quad \rightarrow \quad \begin{array}{l} \text{While } N_{(1)} \text{ is } V_1{-}ing \\ N_{(2)} \text{ is } V_2{-}ing \end{array}$$

The resultant sentence may also have the form

$$N(_1) \quad V_1\text{--}t \quad \text{əstana} \quad N(_2) \quad V_2\text{--}t \quad Aux$$

तो काम करीत आहे.

to kam kərit ae.
He is working.

त्यावेळेला तो गाणं म्हणत आहे.

tyaveḷela to gaṇə: mhəṇət ae.
At that time he is singing.

तो काम करताना गाणं म्हणत आहे.

to kam kərtana gaṇə: mhəṇət ae.
He is singing while he is working.

एक बाई साफ–सफाई करीत आहे.

ek bai saph–səphai kərit ae.
One woman is cleaning.

त्यावेळेला दुसरी बाई स्वैपाक
करीत आहे.

tyaveḷela dusri bai svəipak
kərit ae.

At that time the other woman
is cooking.

एक बाई साफ–सफाई करीत
असताना दुसरी बाई स्वैपाक
करीत आहे.

ek bai saph–səphai kərit
əstana dusri bai svəipak
kərit ae.

While one woman is cleaning
the other is cooking.

The original pair of sentences may also be in the imperfect A.

$$\begin{array}{l} N_1 \quad V_1\text{--}t\text{--}E \\ \textit{tyaveḷela } N(_2) \quad V_2\text{--}t\text{--}E \end{array} \rightarrow N(_1) \quad V_1\text{--}\textit{tana} \quad N(_2) \quad V_2$$

$$\begin{array}{l} N_1 \quad V_1 \\ \text{At that time} \quad N(_2) \quad V_2 \end{array} \rightarrow \text{While } N(_1) \quad V_1 \quad N(_2) \quad V_2$$

तो काम करतो.

to kam kərto.
He works.

त्यावेळेला तो गाणी म्हणतो.

tyaveḷela to gaṇi mhəṇto.
At that time he sings.

तो काम करताना ( करीत असताना )
गाणी म्हणतो.

to kam kərtana ( kərit əstana )
gaṇi mhəṇto.

He sings while working.

एक बाई साफ-सफाई करते.      ek bai saph–səphai kərte.

One woman cleans.

त्या वेळेला दुसरी बाई स्वैपाक करते.      tya veḷela dusri bai svəipak kərte.

At that time the other does
the cooking.

एक बाई साफ–सफाई करताना ( करीत      ek bai saph–səphai kərtana ( kərit
असताना ) दुसरी बाई स्वैपाक करते.      əstana ) dusri bai svəipak kərte.

While one woman cleans, the other
does the cooking.

( ii ) *V–tana* may also be used to embed a sentence as the direct object of
another, according to the formula below.

$$N_1 \quad V–t \quad Aux$$
$$tyaveḷela \quad N_2 \quad N_1 \quad pah– \qquad \rightarrow \quad N_2 \quad N_1 \quad V–tana \quad pah–$$
$$əik– \qquad\qquad\qquad\qquad\qquad\qquad\qquad\qquad\qquad əik–$$

$$N_1 \quad is \quad V–ing$$
$$At \quad that \quad time \quad N_2 \quad see– \quad N_1 \qquad \rightarrow \quad N_2 \quad see– \quad N_1 \quad V–ing$$
$$hear– \qquad\qquad\qquad\qquad\qquad\qquad\qquad\qquad\qquad hear–$$

तो काम करीत होता.      to kam kərit hota.

He was working.

त्या वेळेला मी त्याला पाहिलं.      tyaveḷela mi tyala pahilə:.

I saw him at that time.

तो काम करताना मी त्याला पाहिलं.      to kam kərtana mi tyala pahilə:.

I saw him while he was working.

( iii ) *V–tana* may also be used if one of the sentences has only an auxiliary
verb.

$$N_1 \quad V$$
$$tyaveḷela \quad N_{(2)} \quad Adv. \quad Aux \qquad \rightarrow \quad N_{(2)} \quad Adv. \quad əstana \quad N_1 \quad V$$

$$N_1 \quad V$$
$$At \quad that \quad time \quad N_{(2)} \quad be– \quad Adv \qquad\qquad \rightarrow \quad While \quad N_{(2)} \quad be– \quad Adv. \quad N_1 \quad V$$

तो आला.      to ala.

He came.

त्यावेळेला मी बाहेर होतो.      tyaveḷela mi baher hoto.

At that time I was out.

मी बाहेर असताना तो आला.

mi baher əstana to ala.
He came while I was out.

तो अमेरिकेत होता.

to əmeriket hota.
At that time he was in America.

त्यावेळेला त्यानी खूप कारखाने पाहिले.

tyaveḷela tyani khup karkhane pahile.
He saw many factories.

अमेरिकेत असताना त्यानी खूप कारखाने पाहिले.

əmeriket əstana tyani khup karkhane pahile.

While he was in America he saw many factories.

(8) *V-t*. A pair of sentences of the form below may combined into a single sentence.

$$\begin{array}{l} N \ V_1 \\ tyave\d{l}ela \ N \ V_2\text{--}t \ Aux \end{array} \quad \rightarrow \quad N \ V_2\text{--}t \ V_1$$

$$\begin{array}{l} N \ V_1 \\ \text{At that time} \ N \ be\text{--} V_2\text{--}ing \end{array} \quad \rightarrow \quad N \ V_1 \ V_2\text{--}ing$$

Note that the subject must be the same in the two sentences.

तो बिरबलकडे गेला.

to birbəlkəḍe gela.
He went to Birbal.

त्यावेळेला तो रडत होता.

tyaveḷela to rəḍət hota.
At that time he was crying.

तो रडत बिरबलकडे गेला.

to rəḍət birbəlkəḍe gela.
He went crying to Birbal.

आम्ही फिरायला गेलो.

amhi phirayla gelo.
We went for a walk.

त्यावेळेला आम्ही गप्पा मारीत होतो.

tyaveḷela amhi gəppa marit hoto.
At that time we were chatting.

आम्ही गप्पा मारीत फिरायला गेलो.

amhi gəppa marit phirayala gelo.
We went for a walk chatting.

To emphasize the fact that the two actions continued over the same space of time, *V–t* may be repeated.

आम्ही गप्पा मारीत मारीत फिरायला          amhi gəppa marit marit phirayla
गेलो.                                    gelo.

(9) *V–ta V–ta.* A pair of sentences of the form below may be combined into a single sentence.

$$N_1 \ V_1\text{--}t \ Aux$$
$$tyaveḷela \ N_{(2)} \ V_2 \quad \rightarrow \quad N_1 \ V_1\text{--}ta \ V_1\text{--}ta \ N_{(2)} \ V_2$$

$$N_1 \ be\text{--} \ V_1\text{--}ing$$
$$\text{At that time } N_{(2)} \ V_2 \quad \rightarrow \quad \text{While } N_1 \ be \ V_1\text{--}ing \ N_{(2)} \ V_2$$

Note that this construction has nearly the meaning as *V–tana.* Also like *V–tana,* it does not require that the subject of the two sentences be identical. *V–ta V–ta,* however, is less commonly used than *V–tana.*

आम्ही बोलत होतो.                         amhi bolət hoto.
                                         We were talking.

एक विषय निघाला.                          ek višəy nighala.
                                         A subject came up.

आम्ही बोलता बोलता एक                     amhi bolta bolta ek
विषय निघाला.                             višəy nighala.

                                         As we were talking, a subject
                                         came up.

जावईबुवा भुरका मारीत होते.               javəibuva bhurka marit hote.
                                         The son–in–law was slurping.

त्यावेळेला त्यांनी उत्तर दिलं.           tyaveḷela tyanni uttər dilə:.
                                         At that time he answered.

भुरका मारता मारता जावईबुवांनी            bhurka marta marta javəibuvanni
उत्तर दिलं.                              uttər dilə:.

                                         Slurping, the son–in–law answered.

(10) *V–tac.* A pair of sentences of the form below may be combined into a single sentence.

$$N_1 \ V_1$$
$$ləgec \ N_{(2)} \ V_2 \quad \rightarrow \quad N_1 \ V_1\text{--}tac \ N_{(2)} \ V_2$$

$$N_1 \ V_1$$
$$\text{Immediately } N_{(2)} \ V_2 \quad \rightarrow \quad \text{As soon as } N_1 \ V_1 \ N_{(2)} \ V_2$$

| | |
|---|---|
| दिवस उजाडला. | divəs ujaḍla. |
| | Day dawned. |
| लगेच तो बाहेर निघाला. | ləgec to baher nighala. |
| | Immediately he set out. |
| दिवस उजाडताच तो बाहेर निघाला. | divəs ujaḍtac to baher nighala. |
| | As soon as day dawned he set out. |

( 11 ) *nə: V–ta*. A pair of sentences of the form below may be combined into a single sentence.

$$\begin{matrix} N\ V_1 \\ N\ V_{2\ neg} \end{matrix} \quad \rightarrow \quad nə:\ V_2\text{–}ta\ N\ V_1$$

$$\begin{matrix} N\ V \\ N\ V_{2\ neg} \end{matrix} \quad \rightarrow \quad N\ V_1\ \text{without}\ V_2\text{–ing}$$

| | |
|---|---|
| ती घरी राहिली. | ti ghəri rahili. |
| | She stayed at home. |
| ती शाळेत गेली नाही. | ti šaḷet geli nahi. |
| | She didn't go to school. |
| शाळेत न जाता ती घरी राहिली. | šaḷet nə jata ti ghəri rahili. |
| | She stayed at home without going to school. |
| त्यानी पगार घेतला. | tyani pəgar ghetla. |
| | He took the salary. |
| त्यानी काम केलं नाही. | tyani kam kələ: nahi. |
| | He didn't do the work. |
| काम न करता त्यानी पगार घेतला. | kam nə: kərta tyani pəgar ghetla. |
| | He took the salary without working. |

( 12 ) *V– aycya + post*. A pair of sentences of the form below may be transformed into the sentence.

$$\begin{matrix} N_1\ V_1 \\ tya\text{–}əgodər\ N_{(2)}\ V_2 \\ purvi \\ adhi \end{matrix} \quad \rightarrow \quad N_1\ V_1\text{–}aycyaəgodər\ N_{(2)}\ V_2$$

$$\begin{matrix} N_1\ V_1 \\ \text{Before that } N_{(2)}\ V_2 \end{matrix} \quad \rightarrow \quad \text{Before } N_1\ V_1,\ N_2\ V_2$$

| ती येईल. | ti yeil |
|---|---|
| | She will come. |

| त्याअगोदर आम्हाला हे काम संपवलं पाहिजे. | tyaəgodər amhala he kam səmpəvlə̃: pahiǰe. |
| | Before that we have to finish this work. |

| ती यायच्याअगोदर आम्हाला हे काम संपवलं पाहिजे. | ti yayčyaəgodər amhala he kam səmpəvlə̃: pahiǰe. |
| | Before she comes we have to finish this work. |

| आम्ही इथे आलो. त्याअगोदर आम्ही मुंबईला दहा दिवस राहिलो. | amhi ithe alo. tyaəgodər amhi mumbəila dəha divəs rahilo. |
| | We came here. Before that we stayed in Bombay for ten days. |

| इथे यायच्याअगोदर आम्ही दहा दिवस मुंबईला राहिलो. | ithe yayčyaəgodər amhi dəha divəs mumbəila rahilo. |
| | Before coming here we stayed in Bombay for ten days. |

əivəǰi 'instead of' may also be used in this construction.

| बसनी जाऊ नका. त्याऐवजी* आगगाडीनी जा. | bəsni jau nəka. tyaəivəǰi aggaḍini ja. Don't go by bus. Instead of that go by train. |
|---|---|

| बसनी जायच्याऐवजी आगगाडीनी जा. | bəsni jayčyaəivəǰi aggaḍini ja. Instead of going by bus, go by train. |
|---|---|

## 5. Conditional

( 1 ) *jər tər*. A conditional construction is a special type of relative construction in which the first sentence is a condition of the second. In Marathi the most commonly used form of the conditional construction is:

$$( jər )\ S_1\ tər\ S_2 \qquad\qquad \text{If } S_1 \text{ then } S_2$$

*jər* is often omitted; *tər* may not be omitted.

---

*Note that *əivəǰi* follows a negative verb. The negative form does not occur in the resultant sentence, but is implied by *əivəǰi*.

There are several possibilities as to the permissible verb sequences in a conditional construction.

( a ) $V_1$ and $V_2$ may both be in the future.

(जर) तू जाशील तर मीही जाईन.     (jər) tu jašil tər mihi jain.

If you will go I will too.

( b ) The same meaning as above is more often expressed colloquially with $V_1$ in the perfect. If the first verb is in the imperfect it may be used with the auxiliary in the perfect.

(जर) तू गेलास तर मीही जाईन.     (jər) tu geļas tər mihi jain.

If you go I will too.

(जर) त्यानी हे केलं तर बरं होईल.     (jər) tyani he kelə: tər bərə: hoil.

It will be good if he does it.

If there is an auxiliary in the original sentence, it may be used in the perfect.

(जर) तू मुंबईला जाणार असलास तर माझ्यासाठी एक काम करशील का ?     (jər) tu mumbəila jaṇar əslas tər majhyasaṭhi ek kam kəršil ka ?

If you are going to Bombay will you do something for me ?

(जर) तुला बरं वाटत नसलं तर घरी जाऊन झोप.     (jər) tula bərə: vaṭət nəslə: tər ghəri jaun jhop.

If you don't feel well, go home and sleep.

(जर) सिमेंट जास्त महाग असलं तर आपण चुना वापरू.     (jər) simeṇt jastə məhag əslə: tər apəṇ cuna vapru.

If cement is too expensive we will use lime.

( c ) In the above examples the perfect is used for $V_1$ although the action has not actually occurred. There are also instances in which the action of $V_1$ has occurred, e. g.:

(जर) त्याला परीक्षा अवघड वाटली तर मला नक्की अवघड वाटेल.     (jer) tyala pəriksa əvghəḍ vaṭli tər məla nəkki əvghəḍ vaṭel.

If he found the examination difficult, I definitely will.

(जर) त्यांनी हे केलं तर आम्हीही
करू शकू.

(jər) tyanni he kelə: tər amhihi
kəru šəku.

If he did it so can we.

( d ) *V–lyas*. In writing, a more formal conditional construction is sometimes used.

$$N_1 \quad V_2\text{–}lyas \quad S_2 \qquad \text{If } S_1 \text{ (then) } S_2$$

आता पाऊस पडल्यास पिकांचं
नुकसान होईल.

ata paus pədlyas pikancə:
nuksan hoil.

If it rains now, the crops will be damaged.

## 6. Hypothetical conditional

( 1 ) *V–l–E əs–t–E*. Some conditional sentences postulate a hypothetical situation: if *x* had happened, then *y* would have happened. These are often termed 'contrary-to-fact sentences.' In this book they are referred to as the *hypothetical conditional*. The usual hypothetical conditional sentences have the form:

$$(jər) \; N_1 \quad V_1\text{–}l\text{–}E \quad əs\text{–}t\text{–}E \quad tər \quad N_{(2)} \quad V_2\text{–}l\text{–}E \quad əs\text{–}t\text{–}E$$

$$\text{If } N_1 \text{ had } V_1\text{–ed then } N_{(2)} \text{ would have } V_2\text{–ed}$$

*E* is the regular adjective ending and follows the normal rules for agreement in the perfect.

(जर) ते आले असते तर हे झालं नसतं.

(jər) te ale əste tər he jhalə: nəstə:.

If he had come this wouldn't have happened.

(जर) त्यांनी अभ्यास केला असता
तर तो नापास झाला नसता.

(jər) tyani əbhyas kela əsta tər to
napas jhala nəsta.

If he had studied he wouldn't have failed.

(जर) त्यांनी खत टाकलं असतं तर
पीक चांगलं झालं असतं.

(jər) tyani khət ṭaklə: əstə: tər
pik caŋglə: alə: əstə:.

If he had applied fertilizer the crop would have turned out well.

(जर) पैसे मिळाले असते तर
आम्हाला काम करता आलं असतं.

(jər) pəise miḷale əste tər
amhala kam kərta alə: əstə:.

If we had received the money
we would have been able to
do the work.

( 2 ) **Archaic hypothetical conditional.** There is an archaic form of the hypothetical conditional, which is still sometimes used, though it is limited to the second and third persons. This form is generally used in the first clause of the conditional sentence. In the second clause the normal $V–l–E$ $əs–t–E$ construction is used. Thus the sentence has the form:

$$( jər)\ \ N_1\ \ \ V_2–t–E_{ahc}\ \ \ tər\ \ \ N_{(2)}\ \ \ V_2–l–E\ \ əs–t–E$$

$$\text{If } N_1 \text{ had } V_1–\text{ed then } N_2 \text{ would have } V_2–\text{ed}$$

$E_{ahc}$ stands for the set of archaic hypothetical conditional endings shown in Table 9.1.

Table 9.1.  *Archaic hypothetical conditional endings*

|   | Person | | | Singular | | Plural |
|---|---|---|---|---|---|---|
|   | M | F | N | M | F | N |
| 1 | – | – | – | – | – | – |
| 2 | –as | –is | – | –e | –ya | – |
| 3 | –a | –i | –ə: | –e | –ya | –i |

Note that the third person endings are the regular adjective endings.

ती वेळेवर काम करती तर आई तिला
रागावली नसती.

ti veḷevər kam kərti tər ai tila
ragəvli nəsti.

If she had done  her work on
time her mother would not have
gotten angry with her.

ते स्वतः तिकडे जाते तर काय झालं ते
त्यांना कळलं असतं.

te svətəhə tikḍe jate tər kay jhalə: te
tyanna kəḷḷə: əstə:.

If he had gone there himself he
would have realized what had
happened.

## 7. Concessive

( 1 ) *jəri təri*. The concessive is a special type of relative construction, having the form:

| ( *jəri* ) $S_1$ *təri* $S_2$ | Although $S_1$ $S_2$ |
|---|---|
| (जरी) आम्ही त्यांना खूप सांगितलं तरी ते हायब्रिड ज्वारी लावायला तयार नव्हते. | (jəri) amhi tyanna khup saŋgitlə: təri te haybriḍ jvari lavayla təyar nəvhte. |
|  | Although we tried to persuade them, they were not ready to plant hybrid jowar. |
| (जरी) त्यांची परिस्थिती चांगली आहे तरी त्यांच्या आहारामधे पुरेसे नत्रयुक्त पदार्थे नसतात. | (jəri) tyanči pəristhiti caŋgli ae təri tyancya aharamədhe purese nətrəyuktə pədarthə nəstat. |
|  | Although they are well off, there is not enough protein in their diet. |

The present auxiliary may be replaced by the perfect.

| (जरी) त्यांची परिस्थिती चांगली असली तरी | (jəri) tyanči pəristhiti caŋgli əsli təri |
|---|---|

( 2 ) *ka hoina pəṇ*. The phrase *ka hoina pəṇ* is used in concessive sentences meaning ' though it may be only..., still $S_2$. '

| रोज थोडा का होईना पण व्यायाम केलेला बरा. | roj thoḍa ka hoina pəṇ vyayam kelela bəra. |
|---|---|
|  | One should exercise at least a little (though it may only be a little) every day. |
| रोज चार ओळी का होईना पण वाचल्याशिवाय मी झोपत नाही. | roj čar oḷi ka hoina pəṇ vaclyašivay mi jhopət nahi. |
|  | It might be only four lines, but I never go to sleep without reading. |

## C. Comparison of Sentences

### 1. Comparison of adjectives

( 1 ) **Comparative**. What is usually termed 'comparison of adjectives' is actually comparison of two or more sentences of the form 'N is A', or, in Marathi, $N \; A \; Aux$. A pair of sentences of the form below may be combined into a single sentence.

$$N_1 \; A \; Aux$$
$$N_2 \; jast\partial \; A \; Aux \qquad \rightarrow \quad N_2 \; N_1\text{-} \; pek\check{s}a \; A \; Aux$$

$$N_1 \; \text{is} \; A$$
$$N_2 \; \text{is more} \; A \qquad \rightarrow \quad N_2 \; \text{is more} \; A \; \text{than} \; N_1$$

सी. एस. एच. वनपेक्षा वसंत हायब्रिड      si es eč vənpekša vəsənt haybriḍ
जास्त चांगली आहे.      jastə caŋgli ae.

Vasant hybrid is better than CSH–1.

( 2 ) **Equality**. A pair of sentences of the form below can be combined into a single sentence.

$$N_1 \; A \; Aux$$
$$N_2 \; tevdh\text{-}E \; A \; Aux \qquad \rightarrow \quad N_2 \; N_1\text{-}itk\text{-}E \; A \; Aux$$

$$N_1 \; \text{is} \; A$$
$$N_2 \; \text{is equally} \; A \qquad \rightarrow \quad N_2 \; \text{is as} \; A \; \text{as} \; N_1$$

$E$ is the regular adjective ending and agrees with $N_2$.

ही जात त्या जातीइतकीच चांगली आहे.  hi jat tya jati-itkic caŋgli ae.

This variety is as good as that.

हा डोंगर त्या डोंगराइतका उंच आहे.  ha ḍoŋgər tya ḍoŋgra–itka uncə ae.

This hill is as high as that one.

( 3 ) **Superlative**. The superlative is the result of the comparison of three or more sentences of the type $N \; A_1 \; Aux$. The resultant sentence has the form:

$$(N_{123}\text{-}p\partial iki) \; N_3 \; s\partial g\underset{.}{l}yat \; A \; Aux$$

(Of $N_{123}$) $N_3$ is the most A of all

(वर्गातल्या मुलांपैकी) ती सगळ्यांत      (vərgatlya mulampəiki) ti səglyat
हुशार आहे.      hušar ae.

( Of the children in the class ) she is the brightest.

( ह्या भागातल्या डोंगरांपैकी )          (hya bhagatlya ḍoŋgrampəki)
हा डोंगर सगळ्यांत उंच आहे.              ha ḍoŋgər səgḷyat uncə ae.

                                        (Of the hills in this area)
                                        this hill is the highest.

त्यानी लिहिलेल्या पुस्तकांपैकी          tyani lihilelya pustəkampəiki
हे पुस्तक सर्वांत चांगलं आहे.           he pustək sərvat caŋglə: ae.

                                        Of the books he has written
                                        this one is the best.


## 2.  Comparison of N V sentences

( 1 ) Sentences of the form  *N  V*  can be compared in  the  same  manner  as
*N A Aux* sentences. It is  not  necessary  to  give  formulas  for  these;  examples
should suffice.

इतर धान्यांपेक्षा महाराष्ट्रातील        itər dhanyampekša məharaštratil
लोक जास्त ज्वारी खातात.                lok ˇjastə ˇjvari khatat.

                                        People in Maharashtra eat more
                                        jowar than any other grain.

हिमालयात युरोपइतकी थंडी पडते.          himaləyat yuropitki thəṇḍi pədte.
                                        It gets as cold in the Himalayas as it
                                        does in Europe.

( 2 ) *V–ṇyaitk– E A.*  The construction *V–ṇyaitk – E A* means ' A enough
to V. '

मला भाषण करण्याइतकं मराठी येत नाही.    məla bhašəṇ kərṇyaitkə: məraṭhi
                                        yet nahi.

                                        I don't know enough Marathi
                                        to make a speech.

तो रणांगणामधे उडी घेण्याइतका            to rəṇaŋgəṇamədhe uḍi gheṇyaitka
शूर असतो.                              šur əsto.

                                        He is brave enough to jump onto
                                        the battlefield.

# Chapter ten

# VERBAL NOUNS AND ADJECTIVES

The Marathi verbal nouns and adjectives are constantly used and are an essential part of the structure of the language. They do not, however, easily lend themselves to the transformational framework used in this book. Therefore they have been treated in a separate chapter. Future work, however, will undoubtedly clarify how they fit in a transformational framework.

1. *V–nə:*

The Marathi verbal noun *V–nə:** is similar to the English 'to V' or 'V–ing'. It may be thought of as a generalization of a verbal action.

Usually when a verb is cited, it is given in this form: *kərnə:* 'to do', *janə:* 'to go,' etc.

झाड–लोट करणं, झाडांना
पाणी देणं, बाजारात जाणं ही
कामं तो करतो.

jhaḍ–loṭ kərnə: jhaḍanna
paṇi denə:. bajarat janə: hi
kamə: to kərto.

He does jobs of sweeping, watering the trees, and going to the bazar.

प्रदक्षिणा करणं म्हणजे देवळाच्या
भोवती फेरी मारणं.

prədəkšiṇa kərṇə: mhən̄je
devḷaćya bhovti pheri marṇə:.

Doing *pradakshina* means going round the temple.

असं करणं चांगलं नसतं.

əsə: kərṇə: caŋglə: nəstə:.
It is not good to do something like that.

*In writing and in formal speech, *V–ṇe* is used.

**167**

Since *V–nə:* is a noun, it may in some cases be made plural.   Note  that it is neuter.

त्यांची जाणी येणी सारखी होतात.          tyanči jaṇi yeṇi sarkhi hotat.

They constantly come and go.

( Lit., ' their comings and
goings constantly occur. ' )

त्यांनी लोकांना बोलावणी पाठवली.          tyani lokanna bolavṇi paṭhəvli.

He sent invitations to people.

This form is also used for a formal request.

पांडुरंग आढाव ह्यांना          paṇḍurəŋg aḍhav hyanna

रु. १५०० चा चेक देणे.          ru pəndhrašeca ček deṇe.

Please give Pandurang Adhav
a check for Rs. 1500.

2.    *V–nya + post.*   *V – nə:* is also used with postpositions in a variety of constructions.

( 1 ) *V–nya + purvi / əgodər / adhi, etc.*   In this construction   *V–nya–*   is interchangeable with    *V– aycya–.*

काम सुरू करण्यापूर्वी लेखी          kam suru kərṇyapurvi lekhi noṭis
नोटीस पाठवा.          paṭhva.

Before beginning work, send a
written notice.

( 2 ) *V–nya + saṭhi / kərta.*   This   construction   is   interchangeable   with   *V–ayla.*

मंत्र्यांना भेटण्यासाठी ते मुंबईला          məntryanna bheṭṇyasaṭhi te mumbəila
गेले आहेत.          gele aet.

He has gone to Bombay to meet the
minister.

( 3 ) *V–ṇyas.* *V–ṇyas*   is interchangeable with   *V–ayla.*

असं करण्यास काही हरकत नाही.          əsə: kərṇyas kahi hərkət nahi.

There is no objection to doing this.

( 4 ) *V–ṇyane.* *V–ṇyane*   is often interchangeable with   *V–lyane.*

आपल्या येण्याने आम्हाला आनंद झाला. aplya yeṇyane amhala anəndə jhala.

We are happy you came.

( 5 ) *V–ṇyaprəmaṇe*

तू वडलांच्या सांगण्याप्रमाणे कर.　　tu vədlančya saŋgnyaprəmaṇe kər.

　　　　　　　　　　　　　　　　　　·Do as your father has told you.

( 6 ) *V–ṇyacə:*. With the postposition *cə: V–ṇə:* actually becomes a verbal adjective equivalent to *V–aycə:* and freely interchangeable with it. For the use of *V–aycə:* as a verbal adjective see the following section.

असं होण्याची फारशी शक्यता नाही.　　əsə: hoṇyači pharši šəkyəta nahi.

　　　　　　　　　　　　　　　　　　There's not much possibility of that

　　　　　　　　　　　　　　　　　　happening.

( 7 ) A special use of *V– ṇə:* is found in the construction: *V–ṇyasarkh–E N* 'an N worth V–ing' where *E* is the regular adjective ending, agreeing with N.

बघण्यासारखं ठिकाण　　　　　　　bəghṇyasarkhə: ṭhikaṇ

　　　　　　　　　　　　　　　　　a place worth seeing

वाचण्यासारखी पुस्तकं　　　　　　vacṇyasarkhi pustəkə:

　　　　　　　　　　　　　　　　　books worth reading

3. The postposition *sarkhə:* is also used in the construction *V–lyasarkh–E* 'as if V–ed.' The ending *E* follows the normal rules for agreement in the perfect.

मला मेल्यासारखं झालं.　　　　　məla melyasarkhə: jhalə:

　　　　　　　　　　　　　　　　　I felt extremely embarrassed.

　　　　　　　　　　　　　　　　　( Lit., ' I felt as if I were dead. ' )

काहीतरी फुटल्यासारखा आवाज झाला.　kahitəri phuṭlyasarkha avaj jhala.

　　　　　　　　　　　　　　　　　There was a sound as if something

　　　　　　　　　　　　　　　　　had broken.

ही खरी कॉफी असल्यासारखी वाटते.　hi khəri kɔfi əslyasarkhi vaṭṭe.

　　　　　　　　　　　　　　　　　This tastes like real coffee.

4. *V–ayc–E*

( 1 ) *V–ayc–E* 'of V–ing' is used as a verbal adjective with a large set of nouns. The following are only examples.

| सवय | səvəy | habit |
| गरज | gərəj | need |
| इच्छा | iččha | wish |
| जरूर | jərur | need |
| भीती | bhiti | fear |
| प्रयत्न | prəyətnə | attempt |
| बेत | bet | plan |
| व्यवस्था | vyəvəstha | arrangement |

अर्ज करायची काही जरूर नाही.

ərjə kərayči kahi jərur nahi.

There is no need to make an application.

त्यानी ते दुरुस्त करायचा प्रयत्न केला.

tyani te durustə kərayca prəyətnə kela.

He tried (made an attempt) to repair it.

मुलाला अंधारात झोपायची भीती वाटते.

mulala əndharat jhopayči bhiti vaṭṭe.

The child is afraid of sleeping in the dark.

( 2 ) *V–ayc–E* can be used to incorporate a sentence as the direct object of a limited number of verbs. The incorporated sentence and the main sentence must have the same subject. The construction has the form:

$$N_1 \; (N_2) \; V_1\text{–}ayc\text{–}E \; V_2$$

The ending *E* is the normal adjective ending agreeing with $N_2$. If there is no $N_2$ it is neuter singular.

त्यानी भारतात परत जायचं ठरवलं.

tyani bharətat pərət jaycə: ṭhərəvlə:.
He decided to return to India.

काही चुका दुरुस्त करायच्या राहिल्या.

kahi cuka durustə kərayčya rahilya.
Some mistakes remained uncorrected.

तिनी गाणं म्हणायचं सोडलं.

tini gaṇə: mhəṇaycə: soḍlə:.
She gave up singing.

त्यानी काम करायचं अर्धवट टाकलं.

tyani kam kəraycə: ərdhəvəṭ ṭaklə:.
He left his work half done.

5. *V–lyacə*: ' that...V–ed' is used as a complement of a limited set of verbs. These verbs all have to do with apprehending information about an event. Note that in most of the English sentences it is necessary to specify who heard about the event while in the Marathi sentences it is not. Note also that the ending *ə:* is invariant.

तिथे अपघात झाल्याचं कळलं.

tithe əpghat jhalyacə: kəḷlə:.

We heard that an accident had happened there.

मावशीची प्रकृती बरी असल्याचं त्यांनी कळवलं.

mavšiči prəkriti bəri əslyacə: tyanni kəḷəvlə:.

He informed me that my aunt was in good health.

तो परदेशी गेल्याचं समजलं.

to pərdeši gelyacə: səməjlə:.
I learned that he had gone abroad.

धान्यात किडे झाल्याचं आढळून आलं.

dhanyat kiḍe jhalyacə: adhəḷun alə:.

It was discovered that insects had gotten into the grain.

तो इकडे येणार असल्याचं ऐकलं.

to ikḍe yeṇar əslyacə: əiklə:.
We heard that he was coming here.

6. *V–ayla*

*V–ayla* can be translated ' to V.' In addition to its use as a verb operator ( 7.A.1. ). it can be used as a complement of various elements in the sentence.

( 1 ) Many adjectives can take *V–ayla* as a complement.

मराठी शिकायला फारसं अवघड नाही.

mərathi šikayla pharsə: əvghəḍ nahi.
Marathi is not very hard to learn.

ती दिसायला फार चांगली आहे.

ti disayla phar caŋgli ae.
She is very good–looking.

( 2 ) *V–ayla* is also used as the complement of *əs–* in its existential sense.

इथे बसायला जागा नाही.

ithe bəsayla jaga nahi.
There is no room to sit here.

खुरपायला गवत नव्हतं.

khurpayla gəvət nəvhtə:.
There was no grass to hoe.

( 3 ) A limited set of nouns take *V—ayla* as a complement.

त्याला निघून जायला तेवढंच
*निमित्त* पुरतं.

tyala nighun jayla tevḍhɔːc
*nimittə* purtəː.

That's all the excuse he needs to leave.

जायला काही हरकत नाही.

jayla kahi *hərkət* nahi.

There's no reason not to go.

त्यानी बोलायला सुरवात केली.

tyani bolayla *survat* keli.

He began to speak.

इथे काम करायला भरपूर *वाव* मिळतो.

ithe kam kərayla bhərpur *vav* miḷto.

One has a lot of scope to work here.

( 4 ) A limited set of verbs take *V—ayla* as a complement.

रोज तो शेतावर देखरेख करायला
*जातो*.

roj to šetavər dekhrekh kərayla
*jato*.

Every day he goes to the field to
supervise.

रोज ती इथे गप्पा मारायला येते.

roj ti ithe gəppa marayla *yete*.

Every day she comes here to chat.

तो ट्रॅक्टर चालवायला *शिकतो* आहे.

to ṭrækṭer calvayla *siktoe*.

He's learning to drive a tractor.

तो मुलांना पोहायला *शिकवतो* आहे.

to mulanna pohayla *sikəvtoe*.

He's teaching the children to swim.

कापूस उन्हात वाळायला ठेवा.

kapus unhat vaḷayla ṭheva.

Put the cotton in the sun to dry.

इथून नागपूरला जायला चार तास
लागतात.

ithun nagpurla jayla čar tas
*lagtat*.

It takes four hours to go from here to
Nagpur.

मी लालाला गाडी दुरुस्त करून घ्यायला
सांगेन.

mi lalala gaḍi durustə kərun ghyala
*saŋgen*.

I will tell Lala to have the car fixed.

# Chapter eleven

# WORD DERIVATION

Marathi vocabulary contains a great many derived words. A knowledge of the processes of derivation can often enable a student to understand words he has never encountered before.

### A. Noun Derivation

**1. Abstract noun suffixes**

(1) A number of suffixes are used to derive abstract nouns from adjectives.

    (a) *ta*

| | | |
|---|---|---|
| शक्यता | šəkyəta | possibility |
| भिन्नता | bhinnəta | difference |

    (b) *tvə*

| | | |
|---|---|---|
| महत्त्व | məhəttvə* | importance |
| शुभ्रत्व | šubhrətvə | whiteness |

    (c) *pəṇa*

| | | |
|---|---|---|
| मोठेपणा | moṭhepəṇa | greatness |
| शूरपणा | šurpəṇa | bravery |

    (d) *pəṇ*

| | | |
|---|---|---|
| लहानपण | ləhanpəṇ | childhood |
| मोठेपण | moṭhepəṇ | adulthood |

*This word has two *t*'s because the original word *məhət* ends in a *t*.

(e) *i*

| | | |
|---|---|---|
| उंची | unči | height |
| लांबी | lambi | length |

(f) *ye.* With this suffix the vowel of the preceding yllable changes according to the following rules.

| ə → a | i → əi | u → əu |
|---|---|---|
| स्वस्थ | svəsthə | easy |
| स्वास्थ्य | svasthyə | ease, comfort |
| विशिष्ट | višišṭə | special |
| वैशिष्ट्य | vəišišṭyə | speciality |
| सुंदर | sundər | beautiful |
| सौंदर्य | səundəryə | beauty |

(2) *ṇuk.* This suffix is used to derive abstract nouns from verbs.

| | | |
|---|---|---|
| वागणूक | vagṇuk | behavior |
| करमणूक | kərməṇuk | entertainment |

2.  Agentive suffixes

(a) *kər*

| | | |
|---|---|---|
| विणकर | viṇkər | weaver |
| प्रभाकर | prəbhakər | the sun ( maker of brightness ) |

(b) *kəri*

| | | |
|---|---|---|
| शेतकरी | šetkəri | farmer |
| वारकरी | varkəri | pilgrim |

(c) *kar*

| | | |
|---|---|---|
| कलाकार | kəlakar | artist |
| कीर्तनकार | kirtənkar | performer of kirtans |

(d) *k*

| | | |
|---|---|---|
| लेखक | lekhək | writer |
| निरीक्षक | nirikšək | observer |

(e) *gar*

| कामगार | kamgar | workman |
| गुन्हेगार | gunhegar | criminal |

(f) *gir*

| तमासगीर | təmasgir | performer of tamasha |
| कारागीर | karagir | artisan |

(g) *dar*

| दुकानदार | dukandar | shopkeeper |
| वर्गणीदार | vərgəṇidar | subscriber |

(h) *i*

| फिर्यादी | phiryadi | complainant |
| हलवाई | həlvai | sweetmeat seller |

(i) *vala* (var). This suffix indicates any habitutal relationship with the preceding noun.

| दूधवाला | dudhvala | milk–seller |
| लाल केसवाला | lal kesvala | red–haired fellow |

## 3. Feminine suffixes

(a) *in̩*. This suffix can mean either 'wife of N' or 'a woman who is N.'

| माळीण | maḷin̩ | gardener |
| डॉक्टरीण | ḍɔkṭərin̩ | doctor |

(b) *ika*. This suffix means only 'a woman who is N.'

| लेखिका | lekhika | woman writer |
| शिक्षिका | šikšika | woman teacher |

## 4. Other noun suffixes

(a) *khana* 'place'

| दवाखाना | dəvakhana | hospital |
| जिमखाना | jimkhana | sports ground |

(b) *aləy* 'place'

| सचिवालय | səčivaləy | secretariat |
| ग्रंथालय | grənthaləy | library |

( c ) *kər*. This suffix means ' of — (place). When the family moves to a different town it often becomes a surname.

| नगरकर | nəgərkər | Nagarkar |
| पुणेकर | puṇekər | Punekar |

( d ) *kərəṇ*   ' ization '

| औद्योगीकरण | əudyogikərəṇ | industrializtion |
| राष्ट्रीयीकरण | raṣṭriyəkərəṇ | nationalization |

## 5. Reduplication

Marathi makes extensive use of various processes of reduplication.

( 1 ) The most common process is the repetition of a word, with *bi* substituted for the first syllable. This is used to express the idea ' and other such things. ' The original word may be either singular or plural.

| भाज्या | bhajya | vegetables |
| भाज्याबिज्या | bhajyabijya | |
| टेबल | ṭebəl | table |
| टेबलबिबल | ṭebəlbibəl | |
| खुर्च्या | khurčya | chairs |
| खुर्च्याबिच्र्या | khurčyabirčya | |
| अंडी | əṇḍi | eggs |
| अंडीबिंडी | əṇḍibiṇḍi | |

( 2 ) For some words there are special reduplicated forms.

| सामान | saman | collection of objects |
| सामानसुमान | samansuman | |
| उपास | upas | fast |
| उपासतापास | upastapas | |
| नवस | nəvəs | vow to a god |
| नवससायास | nəvəssayas | |

( 3 ) Some words are made up of two different words — often from different languages — meaning the same thing. In most cases the second word is not used independently in Marathi, so for the speaker this is just another form of reduplication. Generally these words also have the meaning ' *x* and such things. '

| दगड | dəgəḍ | rocks |
|---|---|---|
| दगडधोंडे | dəgəḍdhoṇḍe | |
| पैसा | pəisa | money |
| पसाअडका | pəisaəḍka | |
| झाडं | jhaḍə: | trees |
| झाडंझुडपं | jhaḍəjhuḍpə: | |
| कपडा | kəpḍa | clothing |
| कपडालत्ता | kəpḍalətta | |
| गुरं | gurə: | cattle |
| गुरंढोरं | gurə:ḍhorə: | |

( 4 ) The same word may be repeated, sometimes with *ən* ' and ' in the middle.

| आठवडे न् आठवडे | aṭhəvḍen aṭhəvḍe | week after week |
|---|---|---|
| दिबसंदिबस | divəsendivəs | day after day |
| मैल मैल | məil məil | for a whole mile |
| मैलन् मैल | məilən məil | for miles |
| बादली बादलीनी | badli badlini | by the bucket |

## B.  Adjective Derivation

## 1.  Adjectives derived from nouns

( a ) *ik.* A large number of adjectives can be derived from nouns by the addition of the suffix *ik* and the change of the vowel in the preceding syllable according to the rules below.

| ə → a | i → əi | u → əu |
|---|---|---|
| समाज | səmaj | society |
| सामाजिक | samajik | social |
| यंत्र | yəntrə | machine |
| यांत्रिक | yantrik | mechanical |
| इतिहास | itihas | history |
| ऐतिहासिक | əitihaṣik | historical |

| पुराण | puraṇ | mythology |
| पौराणिक | pəuraṇik | mythological |

(b) *i*

| विनोद | vinod | humor |
| विनोदी | vinodi | humorous |
| सरकार | sərkar | government |
| सरकारी | sərkari | governmental |

(c) *iyə*

| शास्त्र | šastrə | science |
| शास्त्रीय | šastriyə | scientific |
| भारत | bharət | India |
| भारतीय | bharətiyə | Indian |

## 2.  Adjectives derived from adverbs

Two suffixes are used for deriving adjectives from adverbs. Both of these suffixes are variant. Note that adverbs having a final *e* drop it before a suffix.

(a) *lə*:

| आत | at | inside |
| आतलं | atlə: | |
| मागे | mage | in back |
| मागलं | maglə: | |
| कुठे | kuṭhe | where |
| कुठलं | kuṭhlə: | |

(b) *cə*:

| मागे | mage | in back, before |
| मागचं | magcə: | |
| आता | ata | now |
| आताचं | atacə: | |
| हल्ली | həlli | at present |
| हल्लीचं | həllicə: | |

3. **Adjectives derived from Sanskrit participles**

( a ) *it.* Adjectives ending in *it* are Sanskrit past participles borrowed into Marathi.

| | | |
|---|---|---|
| आधारित | adharit | based |
| सुशिक्षित | sušikšit | educated |

( b ) *yə.* Adjectives ending in *yə* are Sanskrit future perfect participles borrowed into Marathi.

| | | |
|---|---|---|
| त्याज्य | tyaॅjyə | fit to be given up |
| साध्य | sadhyə | achieveable |

4. **Diminutive and intensive**

Several suffixes may be added to adjectives to modify their force.

( a ) *ṭ*

| | | |
|---|---|---|
| हिरवट | hirvəṭ | greenish |

( b ) *sə:* (var.)

| | | |
|---|---|---|
| लहानसं | ləhansə: | rather small |
| मोठंसं | moṭhəsə: | quite large |

( a ) *sər*

| | | |
|---|---|---|
| लालसर | lalsər | reddish |

( d ) *lə:* (var.)

| | | |
|---|---|---|
| मोठालं | moṭhalə: | big |
| थोरलं | thorlə: | big, elder |

5. **Other adjectival affixes**

( 1 ) **Prefixes**

There are many prefixes which serve an adjectival function in compounds. Some of the most common are listed below.

( a ) *su* ' good '

| | | |
|---|---|---|
| सुविचार | suvičar | good thoughts |

( b ) *ku* ' evil, bad '

| | | |
|---|---|---|
| कुमार्ग | kumargə | evil path |

( c )  *əlpə*  ' few, little '

अल्पसंख्य              əlpəsəŋkhyə            minority

( d )  *bəhu*  ' many '

बहुसंख्य               bəhusəŋkhyə            the majority

( e )  *məha*  ' great '

महाराजा               məharaja              king

( f )  *səmə*  ' same, like '

समांतर                səmantər              parallel

( g )  *səhə*  ' co- '

सहकार्य               səhəkaryə             cooperation

( h )  *punər*  ' re-'

पुनर्जन्म              punər jənmə           rebirth

( i )  *gətə*  ' past '

गतकाल                 gətəkal               the past

( j )  *pərə*  ' foreign, other '

परलोक                 pərəlok               the other world

( k )  *purvə*  ' earlier '

पूर्वार्ध             purvardhə             the first half

( l )  *uttər*  ' latter, later '

उत्तरार्ध             uttərardhə            the latter half

( m )  *nəvə*  ' new '

नवचित्रकला            nəvəčitrəkəla         modern art

( n )  *əgrə*  ' first '

अग्रक्रम              əgrəkrəm              priority

( o )  *upə*  ' sub- '

उपनगर                 upənəgər              suburb

( p )  *mulə*  ' basic '

मूलद्रव्य             mulədrəvyə            element

( q )  *muḷ*  ' original, basic '

मूळगाव                muḷgav                native place

( r )  *pərəmə*  ' greatest, extreme '

परमेश्वर              pərmešvər             God

( s )  *svə*  ' self '

स्वभाव         svəbhav         temperament

Sanskrit numerals are frequently used as prefixes.

( a )  *ekə*  ' one '

एकनिष्ठ         ekəniṣṭhə         devoted to one thing

( b )  *dvi/du*  ' two '

द्वयर्थी         dvyərtɦɪ         having a double meaning

दुप्पट         duppəṭ         double

( c )  *tri*  ' three '

त्रिकोण         trikoṇ         triangle

( d )  *cətur/cətus/cətus̆*  ' four '

चतुष्पाद         čətuš̆pad         four–legged

( e )  *pənčə*  ' five '

पंचमहाभूते         pənčəməhabhute         the five elements

( f )  *s̆əṭ*  ' six '

षट्कोन         š̆əṭkon         hexagon

( g )  *səptə*  ' seven '

सप्तपदी         səptəpədi         ceremony of seven steps

( h )  *əs̆ṭə*  ' eight '

अष्टप्रधान         əš̆ṭəprədhan         council of eight ministers

( i )  *nəvə*  ' nine '

नवनाथ         nəvənath         the nine Naths

( j )  *dəs̆ə*  ' ten '

दशावतार         dəš̆avətar         the ten incarnations

( k )  *s̆ətə*  ' hundred '

शतायुषी         š̆ətayuši         living a hundred years

( l )  *səhəsrə*  ' thousand '

सहस्रभोजन         səhəsrəbhojən         feast for a thousand

( m ) *ləksə* ' hundred thousand '

| | | |
|---|---|---|
| लक्षाधीश | ləkšadhiš | millionaire |

## ( 2 ) Suffixes

There are many adjective suffixes. Some of the most common of them are listed below. These are all invariant.

( a ) *itər* ' non- '

| | | |
|---|---|---|
| ब्राह्मणेतर | bramhənetər | non-Brahman |

( b ) *nisṭhə* ' devoted to , dependent upon

| | | |
|---|---|---|
| बुद्धिनिष्ठ | buddhinišṭhə | intellectual |

( c ) *pər* ' dealing with '

| | | |
|---|---|---|
| पर | bhəktipər | dealing with bhakti |

( d ) *purṇə* ' full of '

| | | |
|---|---|---|
| महत्त्वपूर्ण | məhəttvəpurṇə | important |

( e ) *bhər* ' –ful, -long '

| | | |
|---|---|---|
| बादलीभर | badlibhər | bucketful |
| दिवसभर | divəsbhər | all day long |

( f ) *məy* ' full of '

| | | |
|---|---|---|
| आनंदमय | anəndəməy | happy |

( g ) *šunyə* ' –less '

| | | |
|---|---|---|
| हृदयशून्य | hridəyšunyə | heartless |

( h ) *prədhan* ' predominant '

| | | |
|---|---|---|
| भावनाप्रधान | bhavənaprədhan | sentimental |

( i ) *kšəm* ' capable of '

| | | |
|---|---|---|
| कार्यक्षम | karyəkšəm | competent |

( k ) *bəddhə* ' bound '

| | | |
|---|---|---|
| योजनाबद्ध | yojənabəddhə | planned, deliberate |

( l ) *aspəd* ' -able, –ful '

| | | |
|---|---|---|
| हास्यास्पद | hasyaspəd | laughable |

( m ) *grəstə* ' afflicted by '

| | | |
|---|---|---|
| पूरग्रस्त | purəgrəstə | flood–affected |

( n ) *gət* ' gone '

| | | |
|---|---|---|
| अंतर्गत | əntərgət | internal |

( o ) *man* ' having '

| बुद्धिमान | buddhiman | intelligent |

( p ) *van* ' having '

| विद्वान | vidvan | learned |

( q ) *vəntə* ' having '

| नामवंत | naməvəntə | famous |

( r ) *vəti* (f.) ' having '

| शीलवती | šiləvəti | of good character |

( s ) *məti* (f.) ' having '

| बुद्धिमती | buddhiməti | intelligent |

( t ) *purvə* ' earlier '

| स्वातंत्र्यपूर्व | svatəntryapurvə | before independence |

## 6. Reduplication

The processes of reduplication also apply to adjectives.

( 1 ) The most common process of adjective reduplication is simple repetition. This intensifies the meaning of the adjective.

| जाडजाड | jaḍjaḍ | thick |
| मोठमोठं | moṭhmoṭhə: | big |
| ऊनऊन | unun | hot |
| गारगार | gargar | cold |

( 2 ) For some adjectives there are special reduplicated forms.

| लहान | ləhan | small |
| लहानसहान | ləhansəhan | |
| बारीक | barik | small |
| बारीकसारीक | bariksarik | |
| साधं | sadhə: | simple |
| साधंसुधं | sadhə:sudhə: | |
| म्हातारे | mhatare | old |
| म्हातारीकोतारी | mhatarikotari ( *pl.* ) | |

| खरं | khərə: | true |
| खरंखुरं | khərə:khurə: | |

( 3 ) Some colors have intensifying adjuncts.

| लाल | lal | red |
| लालभडक | lalbhədək | |
| | | |
| हिरवं | hirvə: | green |
| हिरवंगार | hirvə:gar | |
| | | |
| पिवळ | pivḷə: | yellow |
| पिवळधमक | pivḷə:dhəmək | |
| | | |
| पांढरं | paṇḍhrə: | white |
| पांढरंफटक | paṇḍhrə:phətək | |
| | | |
| काळ | kaḷə: | black |
| काळंकुट्ट | kaḷə:kuṭṭə | |

( 4 ) Some words are made up of two different words having the same meaning. In each of the examples given below, the second word is also a commonly used independent word.

| थंडगार | thəṇḍəgar | cold |
| मोठंथोरलं | moṭhə:thorlə: | big |
| फाटकंतुटकं | phəṭkə:tuṭke: | ragged |
| काळंसावळं | kaḷə:savḷə: | dark-skinned |

( 5 ) There are a great number of onomatopoetic adjectives, all employing reduplication. Below are some examples.

| लिबलिबीत | liblibit | gooey |
| लिवलिवीत | livlivit | limp |
| लुसलुशीत | luslušit | tender |
| चुरचुरीत | curcurit | crisp |
| खुसखुशीत | khuskhušit | flaky |
| गिजगिजीत | gijgijit | mushy |
| भुसभुशीत | bhusbhušit | powdery |

| गुलगुळीत | guḷguḷit | polished |
| गुलमुळीत | guḷmuḷit | mumbled, non-committal |
| मिळमिळीत | miḷmiḷit | wishy-washy |
| घसबघशीत | ghəsghəšit | generous |

## C. Relational Affixes

### 1. Negative prefixes

( a ) *ə*

| अन्याय | ənyay | injustice |
| अहिंसा | əhĩvsa | non-violence |

( b ) *nir / nĭs / nis*

| निरपेक्ष | nirapəkšə | disinterested |
| निरक्षर | nirəkšər | illiterate |

( c ) *ən*

| अनपेक्षित | ənəpekšit | unexpected |
| अनिष्ट | əništə | undesirable |

( d ) *dur / dus / dŭs*

| दुर्गम | durgəm | difficult of access |
| दुष्प्रवृत्ती | dušprəvritti | bad tendency |

( e ) *əpə*

| अपकार | əpəkar | bad turn |
| अपयश | əpəyəš | defeat |

( f ) *əvə* 'diminution, lowering'

| अवमूलन | əvəmulən | devaluation |
| अवमान | əvəman | disrespect |

( g ) *nə*

| नावड | navəḍ | dislike |
| नास्तिक | nastik | atheist |

( h ) *na*

| नाइलाज | nailaj | helplessness |
| नापसंती | napəsənti | disapproval |

( i ) *ni*

| निकामी | nikami | useless |
| निगर्वी | nigərvi | modest |

( j ) *gəir*

| गैरसमज | gəirsəməj | misunderstanding |
| गैरसोय | gəirsoy | inconvenience |

( k ) *be* ' without '

| बेताल | betal | uncontrolled |
| बेशरम | bes̆ərəm | shameless |

( l ) *bigər* ' other than, non '

| बिगरमराठी | bigərmərathi | non–Marathi |

( m ) *bin* ' without '

| बिनडोक | bindok | brainless |

( n ) *hin* ' without '

| भूमिहीन | bhumihin | landless |


2. Other relational affixes

( a ) *prəti* ' against '

| प्रतिस्पर्धी | prətispərdhi | competitor |

( b ) *ənu* ' tending towards '

| अनुराग | ənurag | love |
| अनुसरणे | ənusərṇe | to follow |

( c ) *sə* ' with '

| सप्रेम | səprem | with love |

( d ) *ərthə* ' for the purpose of '

| स्मरणार्थे | smərəṇarthə | in memory of |

## D. Verbs

### 1. Transitive verbs

There are a number of regular processes by which transitive verbs are derived from intransitive verbs. The verbs are cited here in the traditional citation form: *V—ṇe*.

( a ) **Change of ə to a.** Note that the transitive verb may have a somewhat divergent meaning.

| | | |
|---|---|---|
| चरणे | cərṇe *v. i.* | to graze |
| चारणे | carṇe *v. t.* | to graze, feed |
| मरणे | mərṇe *v. i.* | to die |
| मारणे | marṇe *v. t.* | to kill, beat |

( b ) **Change of voiceless consonant to voiced.** This may involve vowel change as well.

| | | |
|---|---|---|
| फाटणे | phaṭṇe *v. i.* | to tear |
| फाडणे | phaḍṇe *v. t.* | to tear |
| फिटणे | phiṭṇe *v. i.* | to be repaid |
| फेडणे | pheḍṇe *v. t.* | to repay |

( c ) **Addition of əv.** Tne most common method of deriving transitive verbs is adding *əv* to the verbal base.

| | | |
|---|---|---|
| थांबणे | thambṇe *v. i.* | to stop |
| थांबवणे | thambəvṇe *v. t.* | to stop |
| फिरणे | phirṇe *v. i.* | to spin |
| फिरवणे | phirəvṇe *v. t.* | to spin |

An older variant of *əv* is *əvi*.

| | | |
|---|---|---|
| फिरविणे | phirəviṇe *v. t.* | to spin |

### 2. Causative

( 1 ) When *əv* is added to the base of a transitive verb, the verb becomes a causative. A causative verb is used to indicate an action done through the agency of another.

| आणणे | aṇṇe | to bring |
| आणवणे | aṇəvṇe | to have brought |
| मागणे | magṇe | to ask for |
| मागवणे | magəvṇe | to order |

This also has the older variant *əvi*.

| मागविणे | magəviṇe | to order |

( 2 ) A causative verb used in the imperfect A in an impersonal construction has the meaning ' to be possible to ' or ' to bear to. '

| मला ते बघवत नाही. | məla te bəghvət nahi. |
| | I can't bear to look at it. |

| चल पांडुरंगाच्या पायाशी, | cəl paṇḍurəŋgačya payaši, |
| चालवतं आहे तोवर. | caləvtə:e tovər. |
| | Come on to the feet of Pandurang, while you can still walk. |

The impersonal causative may also be used in the negative habitual.

| मला रहावेना. | məla rəhavena. | I couldn't control myself. |

## 3.   Phrasal verbs

Many actions are expressed in Marathi by a combination of a noun or adjective and *kərṇe;* e. g., *məsagət kərṇe* ' to cultivate. ' To make verbs out of words borrowed from other languages Marathi uses the same device. These verbs may be called *phrasal verbs.*

| काबीज करणे | kabij kərṇe | to seize |
| काबूत येणे | kabut yeṇe | to come within the control of |
| गडप होणे | gəḍəp hoṇe | to disappear |
| खाक होणे | khak hoṇe | to be burned to ashes |
| ऑडजस्ट करणे | ədjəsṭ kərṇe | to adjust |

## 4. Reduplication

Verbs are also subject to various processes of reduplication.

( 1 ) Two verbs of the same meaning are sometimes used together. This construction is restricted to the *V–t* form of the verb.

| धावतपळत | dhavətpəḷət | running |
| मारतझोडत | marətjhoḍət | beating down |

( 2 ) The verb *səvərṇe* is used as an intensifying adjunct with some verbs.

| करूनसवरून | kərunsəvrun | doing |
| शिकलेसवरलेले | šiklesəvərlele | educated and enlightened |

( 3 ) The bare stem of the verb is sometimes repeated to intensify the meaning.

| मारमार मारणे | marmar marṇe | to beat |
| हसहस हसणे | həshəs həsṇe | to laugh |

( 4 ) There are a number of onomatopoetic verbs.

| गुरगुरणे | gurgurṇe | to bark |
| भुरभुरणे | bhurbhurṇe | to sprinkle |
| गडगडणे | gədgədṇe | to crash, tumble |
| फसफसणे | phəsphəsṇe | to rise ( as yeast dough ) |
| फटफटणे | phətphətṇe | to dawn |

## E.   Adverbs

## 1.   Suffixes

( a ) *pəṇe*. Many adverbs of manner are derived from adjectives by the addition of *pəṇe*.

| शांतपणे | šantəpəṇe | calmly |
| स्पष्टपणे | spəštəpəṇe | clearly |

( b ) *pət* ' times over. ' This suffix is used with a preceding numeral to mean ' *x* times over. '

| दसपट | dəspət | ten times over |

## 2. Reduplication

The processes of reduplication are extensively used in Marathi adverbs.

( 1 ) Doublets are common in adverbs of manner. These are of the form *V–un V–un*.

| | | |
|---|---|---|
| येऊनजाऊन | yeunjaun | altogether |
| बोलूनचालून | boluncalun | after all |
| राहूनराहून | rahunrahun | repeatedly, continually |
| घालूनपाडून | ghalunpaḍun | insultingly |
| मारूनमुटकून | marunmuṭkun | forcibly |
| लपूनछपून | ləpunčhəpun | secretly |
| घासूनपुसून | ghasunpusun | immaculately |

( 2 ) There are many onomatopoetic adverbs. Perhaps the largest group of these adverbs are those indicating rapidity or force.

| | |
|---|---|
| ताडकन | taḍkən |
| पटकन | pəṭkən |
| चटकन | cəṭkən |

Many onomatopoetic adverbs use reduplication.

| | | |
|---|---|---|
| सपासप | səpasəp | swiftly, slappingly |
| फटाफटा | phəṭaphəṭa | imitative of fluttering |
| खळाखळा | khəḷakhəḷa | imitative of rattling |
| लटुलटु | luṭuluṭu | imitative of waddling |

## MORPHOPHONEMIC RULES

( 1 ) *Rule M₁*

  $i$ and   $e$   become   $y$   before the addition of   $a$.

   पि + आ = प्या      pi + a = pya
   घे + आ = घ्या      ghe + a = ghya

( 2 ) *Rule M₂*

  $u$   and   $o$   become   $v$   before the addition of   $ə$, $a$   or   $e$.

   नातू + आ = नातवा     natu + a = natva
   हो + आ = व्हा      ho + a = vha*

( 3 ) *Rule M₃*

  $v$   is inserted after $u$ before the addition of   $a$.

   धु + आ = धुवा      dhu + a = dhuva

( 4 ) *Rule M₄*

  The combination of   $a + a$   remains   $a$.
   जा + आ = जा      ja + a = ja

( 5 ) *Rule M₅*

  $c, j, jh$ and   $s$ become respectively $\check{c}, \check{j}, \check{j}h$   and   $\check{s}$ before the addition of   $i$ or $y$.

   त्यांचं पुस्तक      tyacə: pustək
   त्याची गाडी      tyači gaḍi
   त्याचे भाऊ      tyace bhau
   जो माणूस      jo maṇus
   जी माणसं      ǰi maṇsə:
   तो दिवस      to divəs
   त्या दिवशी      tya divši

*This is written and pronounced *vha* instead of the expected *hva*.

( 6 ) *Rule M$_6$*

In a one–syllable word consisting of the sequence CV$_w$ C where V$_w$ is the vowel *i* or *u*, the vowel is shortened before the addition of another vowel.

मीठ + आत = मिठात          miṭh + at = miṭhat

दूध + आत = दुधात          dudh + at = dudhat

( 7 ) *Rule M$_7$*

In a word of two or more syllables ending in the sequence V$_w$CV$_w$C, if the second vowel is *ə, i* or *u* it is deleted before the addition of a vowel. This deletion is not always indicated in writing.

kagəd + a = kagda—

vədil + a = vədla—

sakhər + e = sakhre—

ləsuṇ + a = ləsna—

## SPEECH ETIQUETTE

Speech etiquette in regard to the use of pronouns has already been discussed in 3.C. Here additional information is given about the use of names.

### 1. Men's names

Traditionally in Marathi a man is addressed of referred to by his first name. (There is an important exception: a wife does not use her husband's name. She refers to him with a circumlocution—usually the third person plural pronoun *he*.) To show respect a suffix is added to the name and the plural is used.

The most common suffix for men's names is *rav*. This can be added to almost any name.

| | | |
|---|---|---|
| अरविंद | ərvind | Arvind |
| अरविंदराव | ərvindrav | Arvindrao |

Other suffixes include the following.

| | | | |
|---|---|---|---|
| पंत | pəntə | दादा | dada |
| बुवा | buva* | नाना | nana |
| जी | ji | अण्णा | ənna |
| भाऊ | bhau | | |

| | | |
|---|---|---|
| विष्णुपंत | višṇupənt | Vishnupant |
| सखारामबुवा | səkharambuva | Sakharambuva |
| कृष्णाजी | krišṇaji | Krishnaji |
| हरिभाऊ | həribhau | Haribhau |

These suffixes have a more limited distribution than *rav* and should be used only when one knows that the man in question is referred to that way.

Men are often known by a respectful name different from their given name. This is called a *ṭopəṇnav*. These names are also treated as plural. Some common examples are given below.

| | | |
|---|---|---|
| अप्पासाहेब | əppasaheb | Appasaheb |

*This is usually used for a religious teacher or a classical musician.

193

| नानासाहेब | nanasaheb | Nanasaheb |
| बाळासाहेब | baḷasaheb | Balasaheb |
| भाऊसाहेब | bhausaheb | Bhausaheb |
| काकासाहेब | kakasaheb | Kakasaheb |
| रावसाहेब | ravsaheb | Raosaheb |

If in a particular context one man clearly outranks others he is often referred to and addressed simply as *saheb*.

An uncle is addressed or referred by his name plus a word indicating the relationship. Simply using the name of relationship is also permissible.

| मामा | mama | maternal uncle |
| काका | kaka | paternal uncle |

A father is usually addressed or referred to as *baba*, a grandfather as *ajoba*. *kaka* is often used for any older man.

Tradesmen, especially those who are Gujarati in origin, are often referred to and addressed as *seṭji*.

Along with the traditional method of using names has grown up another style of using the surname. This style is especially associated with government offices, educational institutions, and westernized business. Colleagues usually refer to each other simply by the surname: *sinde, boravke, peṭkar* etc. In referring to their boss, however, they append *saheb*, e. g. *bhoslesaheb*. In addressing the boss directly they usually use only *saheb* or *ravsaheb*. A teacher is usually referred to by his surname with *sər* ' sir ' added: *apṭesər*. He is then addressed simply as *sər*. All these forms are treated as plural.

## 2. Women's names

A woman, like a man, is traditionally referred to by her given name plus a suffix. The suffixes most commonly added are *bai* and *tai*. These may be treated as either plural or singular though more often plural.

| कृष्णाबाई | krišṇabai | Krishnabai |
| सीताबाई | sitabai | Sitabai |
| उषाताई | ušatai | Ushatai |

A woman may also be addressed or referred to simply as *bai* or *tai* without a preceding name.

A female relative is addressed or referred to by her name plus a word indicating the relationship. Simply using the name of the relationship is also permissible.

| ताई | tai | elder sister |
| मावशी | mavši | mother's sister |
| आत्या | atya | father's sister |
| वहिनी | vəhini | elder brother's wife |

Speakers often use these terms for women not actually related to them. Any slightly older woman may be addressed as *mavši*. A bride in a family is addressed as *vəhini* by members of the family and often by outsiders as well. A friend's wife is also called *vəhini*. A woman considerably older may be addressed as *mai* 'mother' or *aji* 'grandmother.' *mai* and *aji* are not usually preceded by a name.

For some women a relational suffix has become part of their name, and almost everyone uses it in reference to them.

In offices and educational institutions, a woman, like a man, is referred to by her surname. The respectful suffix *bai*, however, is often used.


## 3. Intermediate relationships

Normally, use of the first name without a respectful suffix implies the use of the singular. Some speakers, however, make a further distinction between the use of the first name with the singular and the use of the first name with the plural. The use of the first name with the plural is reserved for intermediate relationships halfway between distance and intimacy.

## CONTRAST OF PRESENT AND IMPERFECT A FORMS OF AUXILIARY

The auxiliary əs– 'to be;' is used in the imperfect A form to indicate habitual action. It contrasts with *ahe*, which is used to refer to either a condition obtaining at the present moment or a general truth.

| | |
|---|---|
| ते ऑफिसात आहेत. | te ɔphisat aet. |
| | He is in the office (now). |
| रोज दुपारी ते ऑफिसात असतात. | roj dupari te ɔphisat əstat. |
| | Every afternoon he is in the office. |
| हे पुस्तक फार अवघड आहे. | he pustək phar əvghəḍ ae. |
| | This book is very difficult. |
| त्याची पुस्तकं नेहमी फार अवघड असतात. | tyači pustəkə: nehemi phar əvghəḍ əstat. |
| | His books are always very difficult. |
| त्याचा भाऊ पुण्यात आहे. | tyaca bhau puṇyat ae. |
| | His brother is in Poona (at present). |
| त्याचा भाऊ पुण्यात असतो. | tyaca bhau puṇyat əsto. |
| | His brother is usually in Poona. |
| | His brother lives in Poona. |
| नदीमधे पाणी फार कमी आहे. | nədimədhe paṇi phar kəmi ae. |
| | There is very little water in the river. |
| दर उन्हाळ्यात पाणी कमी असतं. | dər unhaḷyat paṇi kəmi əstə:. |
| | Every summer there's little water. |
| आज खूप थंडी आहे. | aj khup thəṇḍi ae. |
| | It's very cold today. |
| डिसेंबरमधे नेहमी थंडी असते. | ḍisembərmədhe nehemi thəṇḍi əste. |
| | It's always cold in December. |
| हे घर लाकडाचं बनवलेलं आहे. | he ghər lakḍačə: bənəvlelə:e. |
| | This house is made of wood. |
| अमेरिकेमधे सामान्य लोकांची घरं बहुतेक लाकडाची बनवलेली असतात. | əmerikemədhe samanyə lokanči ghərə: bəhutek lakḍači bənəvleli əstat. |

In America common people's houses are usually made of wood.

पाण्यात खूप वाईट जीव-जंतू असतात.

paṇyat khup vaiṭ jiv–jəntu əstat.

There are a lot of harmful organisms in water.

हा फ्रॉक फार महाग आहे.

ha phrɔk phar məhag ae.

This dress is very expensive.

ह्या देशात कपडे फारसे महाग नसतात.

hya deśat kəpḍe pharse məhag nəstat.

In this country clothes aren't very expensive.

त्याचा स्वभाव फार शांत आहे.

tyaca svəbhav phar šantə ae.

He has a very calm disposition.

तो आळशी आहे.

to aḷši ae.

He is lazy.

ही मुलगी फार हुशार आहे.

hi mulgi phar hušar ae.

This girl is very bright.

त्या भागात म्हाताऱ्या लोकांचं प्रमाण जास्त आहे.

tya bhagat mhatarya lokancə: prəmaṇ jastə ae.

In that area there is a large proportion of old people.

कीटकांना सहा पाय असतात.

kiṭəkanna səha pay əstat.

Insects have six legs.

पृथ्वी गोल आहे.

prithvi gol ae.

The earth is round.

## GENERAL CONSIDERATIONS OF WORD ORDER

Most of the points below are found elsewhere in this book, but they are put together here for the sake of convenience.

1. **Subject**. The subject generally precedes the verb. In emphatic sentences, it sometimes follows the verb. This construction should be used with caution, however, as it can easily sound rude.

तुम्ही कुठे चालला ?               tumhi kuṭhe calla ?

कुठे चालला तुम्ही ?               kuṭhe calla tumhi ?

Where are you going ?

A subject that is understood is sometimes omitted.

महाराष्ट्रात ज्वारी खातात.          məharaṣṭrat j̇vari khatat.

In Maharashtra (they) eat jowar.

2. **Direct object**. The direct object follows the subject and precedes the verb.

तो मराठी शिकतो.               to məraṭhi šikto.

He studies Marathi.

3. **Indirect object**. The indirect object precedes the direct object.

तो त्यांना मदत करतो.            to tyanna mədət kərto.

He helps them.

4. **Adverbs and postpositional phrases.** As in English, in Marathi too the position of adverbs and phrases serving as adverbs is less rigidly fixed than that of other elements in the sentence. Generally, however, they precede the noun they modify. If there are several adverbs modifying a verb they generally follow the order: time, manner, means or instrument, place.

मी काल पायी डोंगरावर गेलो.      mi kal payi ḍoŋgravər gelo.

I went up on the hill on foot yesterday.

मी काल एस. टी. ने सातारला गेलो.    mi kal esṭine satarla gelo.

I went to Satara by S. T. bus yesterday.

The relative position of the objects and the adverbs and postpositional phrases depends on what part of the sentence is new information. Compare the following sentences.

काल लायब्ररीमधे मी ते सबंध पुस्तक वाचलं.

kal laybrərimədhe mi te səbəndhə pustək vaclə:.

Yesterday in the library I read the whole book.

(The hearer knows that the speaker was in the library yesterday. The new information is what he accomplished there.)

मी ते पुस्तक लायब्ररीमधे वाचलं.

mi te pustək laybrərimədhe vaclə:.

I read that book in the library.

(The hearer knows that the speaker has read the book. The new information is where he did it.)

# SUBJECT INDEX

## INDEX OF VERB FORMS